STEAL THIS STYLE

STEAL THIS STYLE

MOMS AND DAUGHTERS SWAP WARDROBE SECRETS

LOOKS THAT MAKE HIP CLASSIC AND CLASSIC COOL

SHERRIE MATHIESON

CLARKSON POTTER/PUBLISHERS

NEW YORK

Published in the United States by Clarkson Potter/Publishers,
an imprint of the Crown Publishing Group,
a division of Random House, Inc., New York.
www.crownpublishing.com
www.clarksonpotter.com

Clarkson Potter is a trademark and Potter with colophon
is a registered trademark of Random House, Inc.

Library of Congress Cataloging-in-Publication Data
Mathieson, Sherrie.
Steal this style / Sherrie Mathieson. —1st ed.
     p. cm.
1. Women's clothing. 2. Fashion. 3. Dress accessories. 4. Beauty,
Personal. 5. Mothers and daughters. I.Title.
 GT1720.M37 2009
 391'.2—dc22   2008036986

ISBN 978-0-307-40676-7

Printed in China

Photographs by Nick Saraco

Design by Jennifer K. Beal Davis and Lauren Monchik

10 9 8 7 6 5 4 3 2 1

First Edition

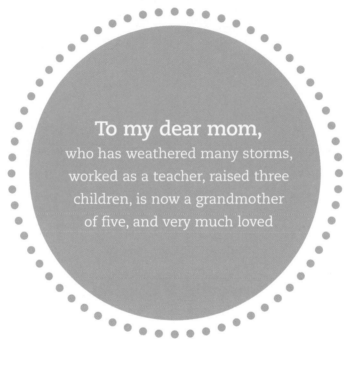

To my dear mom,
who has weathered many storms,
worked as a teacher, raised three
children, is now a grandmother
of five, and very much loved

contents

Introduction—**What Comes Around Goes Around**...1

Meet the Models...8

Chapter One—**Be a Sport!**...16

Chapter Two—**Casual Rules!**...42

Chapter Three—**Work It Out**...102

Chapter Four—**Fancy That!**...134

Chapter Five—**Night Magic**...178

Chapter Six—**Speaking Accessories**...192

Chapter Seven—**The Total Package**...214

Observing Style in Motion: Sources of Inspiration...224

Shopping Around...234

Special Thanks...248

introduction

What Comes Around Goes Around . . .*

"Children get older, I'm getting older, too . . ."
—Stevie Nicks, "Landslide"

No sooner had I donned my hat as a self-appointed casting agent and begun my pursuit of mothers and daughters who met my purpose for this book— moms whose style sense needed reinvention with some fresh ideas from their offspring—than I was met with an almost universal cry for help. This plea resounded not only from the baby boomer moms I interviewed, but also from their hopeful daughters, who furtively confessed that their fondest wish was for their moms to look as good as their daughters knew they could. These young women would gladly leave their closet doors ajar so Mom could steal a choice item or two. If they could just convince her to cross the threshold! And what items? Showing moms what they could take from their daughters' (and in a couple of cases, granddaughters') closets became my mission.

*Hey, sometimes it's a good thing!

Take It with a Twist

One notion that all the moms agreed on was that as we get older we have to navigate some pretty murky fashion waters in search of modern pieces that are right for our age and physicality. After all, we really can't duplicate what our daughters are wearing exactly. It's a matter of degree. The key is to build a bridge between timeless styles and current looks. We do this by first acquiring a collection of core pieces that endure, in ever-changing youthful cuts and color palettes, and then mixing them with a rich variety of accessories (both classic and trendy) that give an intentional nod to what's on the newsstands.

In that spirit, *Steal This Style* is dedicated to exploring the fun enterprise of getting dressed well, with plenty of advice on how to successfully decode the often-illusive current fashion *and* youth scenes. The good news is there's plenty you can take from a variety of younger generations. We might have been the ones who helped start the fashion revolution (not to mention a few others) oh-so-many years ago—the "latest" styles (bootleg jeans, shift dresses) are often taken straight from the pages of our high school yearbooks and reinterpreted. Ironic, isn't it? But why not keep that youthful exuberance alive in our wardrobes?

Our Roots of Style

Think for a moment about where your style began and how it has changed or stalled over the years. Perhaps you started out as I did. As a young girl, I was dressed by my mother, who, given the dictates of the time, was conservative and ladylike in her own look. Unlike today, simple but well-made skirt suits and dresses made from natural fibers such as silk, cotton, and wool were the norm for women in the 1940s and 1950s. My mom, a talented knitter, created adorable, one-of-a-kind outfits for me. She often completed my look with a big satin or grosgrain ribbon in my hair. Today the only children who still wear similarly charming,

stand the beautiful elements of the classic style my mother favored as a young woman. Let's face it: the '60s happened, and, well, wow! All bets were off. My picture album bears witness to my experimentation. It was a challenge for my girl-friends and me to keep up with new styles—so much so it kept us up at night!

The pieces that were coming from designers filled me with aesthetic adrenaline. I had my grandmother, a seamstress, re-create suits I imag-ined Audrey H. and Jackie O. would have worn. In the '70s I embraced hot pants as some do religion. They were often made from suede, or even fully sequined, and extremely abbreviated—the less the merrier (oh, no . . . oh, yes). Those were the days of fakery deluxe. False eyelashes, artificial "falls" (hairpieces), and scarves on the head worn with large gold earrings were all part of the look.

Clothes were my way of showing my creativity and high-fashion bent. I, like many of you, was just "doing my thing"—experimenting and having fun, using myself as a guinea pig and model. Our age and the era gave us a pass on being "appropriate"—even the most out-there fads looked completely suitable. My mother tried to

classic, and custom-looking outfits seem to live on Park Avenue.

My most vivid clothing memories, however, are the ones I created myself. I suspect many of you also took long but memorable detours off the fashion freeway before settling on wherever it is you've arrived now. It took me a while to under-

3

block the doorway (fearing for my safety in these outlandish ensembles) and asked, "You're not really going out that way . . . are you?" Yes, I always did! Funny thing is, you could still be hearing that same fateful question, but it is probably no longer coming from your mother. It may well be your daughter who is now concerned about your look.

The Stylish Art of Translation

This role reversal isn't terribly surprising. A lot of us are confused, and as a result are either stuck in the past or have simply given up and wear what's easy, which is not necessarily what's most flattering. In my work as a style consultant, women clients always ask me, "What is appropriate?"— it's suddenly become important to us again. These motivated women come from a variety of backgrounds, are of different ages, and work in all sorts of occupations and fields. They want clothing solutions that are tailored to their lifestyles, personalities, and changing physiques.

To guide them correctly, I formed a truly workable wardrobe theory grounded in classics, but which also included the habit of constantly reassessing clients' and my own attire to remain totally modern. I abandoned my taste for extreme styles long ago, and, after donating a bale of trendy clothes to charity, I made a mental note of what *never* to revisit (e.g., extremely wide shoulder pads and excessive bling, to name just two). Updated classicism handily provides an ageless look while forming a solid foundation for what I call the art of the mix, or the ability to add in trendier pieces, combine designers, and mingle styles. With this groundwork, any woman can individualize with accessories and separates that express her unique personality and interests.

The art of the mix . . . sounds good, doesn't it? You're no doubt wondering how you make such a wardrobe shift—and where your daughter (or the younger generation) fits in. Well, it starts with observation. Generational interplay keeps us from stagnation. Curiosity keeps our minds fresh and encourages a natural eagerness to grow. This is great news, in my estimation. To that end, why shouldn't you take the time to observe women ten, even twenty, years your junior and "borrow" judiciously from their choices, always translating to suit your body, your age, and your lifestyle?

Consider your personal style afresh every five years—*at least*—and a youthful flair may more easily enter your closet.

When Bad Clothes Happen to Good People

Unfortunately, reinterpreting what the younger generation is wearing leaves the margin for error wide open—and that may be the reason we are reluctant to change. Without a fine understanding of how to take the best and leave the rest, we can easily misinterpret twenty- and thirtysomething style and end up looking even older. We run the risk of appearing either painfully desperate to look young, or silly and immature. On the other hand, we can easily age ourselves by resigning ourselves to wearing the same old, same old.

AARP's invitation to join when you hit fifty doesn't mean you automatically become a charter member of a crazy hat club or a purple boa society. Being a baby boomer does not give you license to don an absurd outfit! Nor is it a signal to turn to those clothing stores that are advertised specifically for our age group. You know the ones: they sell dowdy, boxy, voluminous jackets; pull-on pants; gaudy floral blouses; gauze broomstick skirts; and faux ethnic jewelry. Did you correctly suspect all along that the result is an "instant old" look?

Yes, I know some of you may get compliments on your novelty knits and appliquéd shirts. When we meet each other we want to connect, so we comment on anything we can in order to start a conversation, and often it is the wreath attached to your cardigan or the reindeer dangling from your ears. Don't be fooled by the kind words—they are merely conversational ploys.

Can you consider abandoning those paths in favor of a healthier, and prettier, road? The trip requires a bit of self-indulgence and self-care. Feeling and looking great—and feminine—on a daily basis makes a positive difference in your life. Vanity is good—healthy vanity, that is: the kind that encourages fitness and vitality, and, yes, the desire to keep looking your best. Clothing—how you present yourself to the world—is all part of a

Vanity is good!

well-rounded, balanced, and healthful lifestyle. The enthusiastic pursuit of good looks is definitely something we can borrow from our daughters.

Modus Operandi

Given my experience creating *Steal This Style,* I've seen that daughters are more than willing to share their ideas with their moms. But don't we want to give them something stylishly worthwhile in trade? If you think about it, we pass along more than our genes to our daughters; we are passing along our sense of style, too. In the past we had style icons, famous women who inspired us and taught us about style with their appearance. It's not too late for us to become those women today, for the next generation. Looking modern allows us to connect to the younger generation and pass along to them the beauty of timeless dressing in a fun and spirited way. The message we send should not be in the form of a red and black knit suit, pink and gray velour sweats, or a snowman sweater vest. Let's banish the word "senior," and the looks that conjure the word, from our vocabulary and our closets.

To that end, as you view the Never Cool photos, you may recognize (*ahem*) your neighbor. I use a touch of humor in describing the Never Cool mistakes shown here, with an understanding that these errors are easy to make for all of us because of force of habit, lack of knowledge, utter confusion, and little exposure to good accessible alternatives.

Study the Forever Cool photographs by taking careful notice of how separates are paired and how accessories are mixed together. The looks that the moms and their daughters are wearing rarely come from a single designer or store—their success lies not in a preplanned combination

> **Being a baby boomer does not give you license to don an absurd outfit!**

thought up by a single guru, but in the artful mix of the best-quality ingredients. That's why the Forever Cool ideas and looks presented within these pages are here for the long haul, and wearing them guarantees positive results.

Though it may be tempting, don't just use the book as a fan and flip through it quickly while laughing at the Never Cools. Take the time not just to consider all the photos, but also to read the captions. Find yourself in the Forever Cool styles that apply best to your figure and preferences. Then take the book shopping, or use it while selecting (or clearing out) items from your closet. *Steal This Style* is a tool, and it's the next best thing to me taking you on a shopping trip, something I enjoy doing for clients. Sharing the book with your daughter or a younger friend is a chance to engage her and start a conversation as well. It works: a remarkable thing happened during the making of this book—my duos grew closer *and* more stylish. Clothes are remarkably powerful!

You really can be Forever Cool— forever!

meet the models

The following women so generously gave their time to model for this book—they approached their mission (especially the Never Cool shots) with enthusiasm and good humor. In most cases the women you see are related as mother and daughter (and in a couple of cases, grandmother and granddaughter) in the traditional sense. A few are mother and daughter in spirit—but it does not diminish their close relationship or make it any less meaningful. You'll enjoy getting to know them. In fact, you will hear from many of them in the pages that follow.

Alexis and Susan

Recruiter
Age: 25

School principal
Age: Forever young

Diana and Abby

Special education
teacher
Age: 57

Law student
Age: 22

Michelle and Yasue

Medical student
Age: 21

Administrative
assistant
Age: 50

Daniele and Shenandoah

Realtor
Age: Forever
young

Pianist
Age: 49

Katherine, Kate, and Nancy

Homemaker
Age: 86

Intern at an
architecture firm
Age: 23

Planning and zoning
administrator
Age: 52

Danielle and Paulette

Journalism
student
Age: 24

Dental assistant
Age: 55

Hedy and Mia

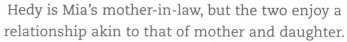

Hedy is Mia's mother-in-law, but the two enjoy a
relationship akin to that of mother and daughter.

Homemaker
Age: 63

Interior design
executive
Age: 36

Cindy and Chris

Realtor
Age: 48

Realtor
Age: 75

Carolyn and Judy

Freelance writer
Age: 35

Office manager
Age: 59

Mimi, Peggy, and Stephanie

Art teacher
Age: 29

University lecturer
Age: 63

Dental hygienist
Age: 34

Gloria and Sally

Psychologist's
assistant
Age: 66

Nursing student
Age: 41

Selina and Jeanne

Technology
consultant
Age: 59

Publicist
Age: 30

Ann and Lura

Certified public
accountant
Age: 53

Philanthropist
Age: 78

Ellen and Mariana

Human resources
executive
Age: 52

Nursing student
Age: 19

Nicole and Ifé

Mother and daughter in spirit—Ifé is friend,
mentor, and adviser to Nicole.

Actress and retail
sales associate
Age: 39

Talent manager
Age: 54

Paige and Portia

Public relations
events specialist
Age: 24

Retired sales
manager
Age: 59

Linda and Laura

Linda is Laura's aunt, but they are as close as a
mother and daughter could be.

Office manager
and paralegal
Age: 57

Boutique sales
manager
Age: 26

Catherine and Allyson

Law student
Age: 22

Travel agency
owner
Age: 46

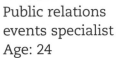

Cynthia and Malene

Life coach
and author
Age: 64

Designer
Age: 34

Kate and Paula

Congressional
legislative
assistant
Age: 23

Bereavement
coordinator
Age: 49

We pass along more than our genes to our daughters....

chapter one
be a sport!

Participation in physical fitness says as much about our youth and vigor as our clothes do. For both mother and daughter, looking appropriate and attractive is also a motivating factor in getting to it—whatever it is. Clothes that can withstand the rigors of our favorite sport or exercise and still flatter the figure are essential. The ever-growing list of high-tech, breathable, lightweight fabrics makes it possible. For workouts like resistance training, aerobics, running, and skiing, fabrics like Malden Polartec Power Dry and Power Stretch have moisture-wicking properties that keep you cool and dry. Modern sporting clothes, whether for golf, hiking, or horseback riding, are now, for the most part, totally ageless, because the best versions keep up with trends in cut and color. They allow for comfort and ease of movement while still providing a pleasing appearance, making it possible to walk away from nearly any activity and still look great right up until dinner. That's right, ladies—today's modern sport clothes are very often worthy of and completely acceptable for walking long city blocks, strolling down Main Street, lunching with friends, or taking in a matinee. Let me show you how to be ready for action with confidence—after all, you want to keep up with your daughter, be it at the gym or on the links.

Off-Kilter

Jeanne's huge top was purchased in her "flower child" days; its stiff cotton encumbers her pose.

Peter Pan Syndrome

Green leggings may have been great in the '80s but are no longer a modern option for Jeanne.

Old Stuff

Those sneaks have seen better days and will definitely inhibit her ability to perform.

FOREVER COOL

Energy Package

Mom Jeanne is at the height of sport chic, wearing high-tech fabric with on-the-go style. Selina, too, is feeling flexible in her easy mix of nylon gear. A spare and clean look is essential, as is the economic and deliberate use of punchy color and sheen.

Survival of the Fittest

Check out the fit on both women. Not too tight or too loose is modern, appropriate, and totally attractive as they go through their day.

Balancing Act

The women's accessories (shoes, watches) are proof positive that form and function are not mutually exclusive.

steal this

Ladies, make sure you have two of everything—even though you could swap, you'll want your own!

Not Pretty in Pink

Underage dressing reinforced by juvenile color choices makes one think, "Wazzup?"

Figured Wrong

Many women who have maintained great figures run a greater risk of inappropriate style.

No Excuses!

Is this a workout outfit?

FOREVER COOL

Triple Threat

Peggy and her two daughters are in perfect form. They wear simple two-piece cotton workout looks in close-fitting, modern cuts. The neutral colors (brown and classic gray) are enhanced by intense hues, like an orange polo or green T-shirt.

Natural Selection

Ponytails, lip gloss, and their natural good looks are all they need for the gym.

Happy Feet

The right sneaker (in great condition) for the activity is also a color adjunct to the outfit.

steal this

A generational swap meet. With similar figures, the style is ageless.

Style Mutiny

With no obvious allegiance to classic boating style, Susan may have to face charges from the naval fashion police. *Kon-Tiki*-meets-sandbox is not the classic and modern look we are after.

Silly Stuff

Take your pick! But those well-known plastic shoes are best in green for gardening, or on grandkids' growing feet.

"People say we are clones. I'm thrilled; my daughter is depressed."
—Susan

FOREVER COOL

Seaworthy

Alexis seizes the perfect opportunity to wear the classic white and navy striped top, with light cotton, white high-cropped pants. Susan (who was blessed with long legs) wears a bright green fitted polo, paired with wide-legged, sailor-inspired, dark navy jeans.

Sure-Footed

Rubber thongs come in many colors and are a warm-weather alternative to classic boating topsiders.

The Right Stuff

Sporty watches and large, bright, utilitarian totes are a boon to any sailor.

steal this

Alexis and Susan can easily trade each other's tops and accessories. The pant styles are both ageless, but each woman wears the style that suits her body.

The Back of the Drawer
Diana threw old clothing together and decided the look was perfect.

Sloppy Style 101
When tucking jeans or pants into boots, make sure to create a smooth line.

Jean Therapy
Does it feel good to have those old faded jeans dig into the waist?

"If I had to order a daughter, she would be Abby."
—Diana

24

FOREVER COOL

First Prize

Diana and Abby exude equestrian style, but its fashion-friendly appeal is comfortable and chic no matter what they're doing. The fitted multibuttoned riding sport jackets, stretch riding pants, and high leather boots all have classic upper-crust nuance. Diana's interpretation is a short, fitted nylon jacket and fitted jeans smoothly tucked into her high rubber boots. Abby is in a fashion version of real riding clothes.

Cohesive Style

Their scarves have an equestrian design theme and finish their outfits beautifully at the neckline.

steal this

It's all about the look itself: ageless and classic. Here Diana wears the perfect combination for her figure. The fitted jeans accentuate the slimness of her legs; the jacket has room and does not demand a perfect torso. Abby could wear mom's pieces, but her outfit should remain in her closet.

Senior Addiction
Would her daughter-in-law dream of
ever wearing this?

Color Me Un-Beautiful
This combination of colors is a
predilection of old folks.

FOREVER COOL

Hitting Par

Modern golf clothes should be sleek, simple, and functional. Leave fussy prints and jarring color choices behind for a winning shot. Mia is crisp in a light, neutral palette, including a white tank layered with a white zip-up sweatshirt and paired with cropped tan pants. Hedy looks great in shades of olive. The long-sleeved polo is practical for easy movement and care. Her cotton pants, cropped low, contribute to a long, lean line.

A Perfect Union

The orange baseball hat and orange-banded sport watch add youthful spirit to Hedy's outfit. The choice of light-colored golf shoes (instead of dark) ensures a "light" feel to both outfits.

steal this

With these outfits, everything is interchangeable. No ID required!

27

Tourist Trap
Persist in choosing tourist shop finds as gym gear?

No Returns
This outfit isn't great anywhere; use your tourist dollars for a spa treatment.

FOREVER COOL

Jump Start

Stay ahead of the game with the right exercise clothes—and, even better, with layers that can carry you stylishly throughout the day. Based on easy black-and-white pieces, a touch of color can be added with a top, jacket, or accessory. Here, mom Cynthia takes a comfortable stance in her thin nylon jacket, which allows the bright yellow of her workout T-shirt to shine through.

Best Picks

Cynthia's glasses are modern in style, work with her features, and are classically suited for sport clothes or a more dressy style. Both Cynthia and daughter Malene chose sneakers that fit their workouts and add a bit of zing to their outfits.

steal this

These are classically oriented workout clothes that are simple in style and ageless in concept. Cynthia and Malene can trade whatever fits.

Bad Sport

Yasue is wearing the same gym togs she's saved from college. Why would she wear them for tennis today?

Worn-out Style

Her whole outfit begs for retirement (but not hers, please!).

"My mom is honestly the only person who is unafraid to tell me how I look in an outfit that just doesn't work."
—Yasue's daughter

FOREVER COOL

Best Score

Yasue and daughter Michelle know that form is as important as function. That's certainly true when both game and style are at issue. Yasue feels pretty in her navy tennis dress (yes, that's when above-the-knee is fine). An argyle sweater over her shoulders adds interest and practicality, should she need warmth off the court. Michelle's classic tennis outfit pairs a fitted polo with a pleated skirt that flatters her curves.

Color That Works

Pairing blues of all intensities and shades with white is as classic as wearing all white. Substitute black for the blues for edgier style.

steal this

Neither woman can go wrong with these classic pieces. Here, mother and daughter are both close in size, and because Yasue is youthful-looking at fifty, they could be just as close in this style.

Take a Hike

Her togs should walk off into the sunset . . . without her!

Needing New Directions

The road to bad style is paved with good intentions. Here only thriftiness prevails.

"Just say no to free clothing offered at technology conferences!"
—Jeanne's daughter

FOREVER COOL

T-Time

Hiking is a great mother-daughter activity, and both look appropriate by keeping it basic (not the same as boring). Trim T-shirts (with a fun graphic for Selina) and flat-front cargo pants are a modern ticket to an easy stride.

Sole Survivor

Both traction and rugged-chic looks come with these hiking sneakers.

> **steal this**
>
> It helps to be close in size, and mom and daughter can share it all, the look . . . and their water.

Running Wild
Animal prints have no place in athletic-looking sport style.

Sloppy Style
Straight from her bed, mom Daniele thinks she's ready to go. Has she forgotten what her own mother taught her?

The Wrong Stuff
Running in platform sneakers will do anyone in.

FOREVER COOL

She Cleans Up Nicely!

No other way to say it: Daniele is movie-star beautiful once she gets it together. Her solid black cashmere "workout" look (with simple white racing stripe) is the answer. A busy day or air travel is a good reason for any woman to wear this upscale yet totally understated look. Daughter Shenandoah can exercise and travel in her version, too.

Seeing Black and White

This quintessential color combo is perfect for an athletic style that stands up to long city jaunts. Keeping their accessories in the same colors adds extra sophistication and edgy style.

steal this

You bet! This style is so basic and ageless that mom and daughter can pack sparingly. Sharing these clothes is as easy as handing them over.

The secret is in having a core look for your physical activities, and perhaps changing a shoe or adding a jacket.

Bigfoot Lives!
Here's proof, if you never believed it.

Frozen in Time
Her sense of style needs to thaw.
Keeping warm is no excuse for cold-
weather clothing that wasn't stylish
even when it was bought.

Childish Stuff
Does she share her accessories with
her grandkids? (Clue: she hasn't any!)

FOREVER COOL

Warming Trend

Après ski, mom Paulette and daughter Danielle still maintain the perfect pace. Their nylon/down coat outfits' monochrome look (black and midnight navy), coupled with their sleek design, give a high-style fashion image to utilitarian skiwear. Danielle wears dark navy straight jeans to echo the look that Paulette achieves with her nylon stirrup pant.

Savvy Accessories

By keeping their knits in the same dark palette, they avoid any cutesy pitfalls. The high-style boots are a take on classic après-ski boot designs.

steal this

Mom's coat and boots are a bit sophisticated and ultrachic for Danielle at her present age; another fifteen years and Danielle can go for it. Everything else—knit caps et al.—is fair game.

Yippee-Kai-Yay-Yo Style
That jacket may outlive us all! It's ubiquitous in the boomer ladies' specialty stores. Wear it and you're branded. Ouch!

Bling Binge
Unless you're singing in Nashville, sequins are not show worthy. Too much bling gives new meaning to the phrase "wild, wild West"!

FOREVER COOL

The Real Deal

If you can corral the urge to overdo, Western wear can be amazingly classic and becoming. The secret is authenticity. Daniele wears a soft deerskin, fringed jacket, a classic Western shirt, brown corduroy jeans, and tan suede Western-style boots. Shenandoah's taller frame is perfect in a tan leather Levi's-style jacket, white Western shirt, dark navy bootleg jeans, and brown flat boots with a Western-feel pointy toe.

The Right "Old" Stuff

Old Native American jewelry (sometimes called Pawn jewelry) is the best complement to this look. A modern artisan's creations that have a similar design (using real silver and stones) can also accessorize a style that is chock-full of creative statement opportunies.

steal this

These classic pieces have survived since the birth of the word "cowboy." So these cowgirls can enjoy each other's clothes (allowing for the right size)—including the fun fringed jacket.

chapter two
casual rules!

Casual style predominates in our culture, which is why I have given it special expanded play in this book. Everyone is informal and laid back today, and that's not necessarily a bad thing. Yet it's also the realm of potentially hideous errors, where casual often gets confused with thoughtlessness in dressing (you've seen it—baggy tee, tattered pants, and too many et ceteras). Once the nine-to-five world no longer beckons and we are left to our own devices—to write that novel, travel to far-flung lands, or just enjoy our own backyards—we should be conscious of not slipping into (literally and psychologically) sloppiness or the notion that anything goes. Casual is also so very relevant when discussing cross-generational style, since casual prevails in every age group, but especially within our daughters' generations (those X-, Y-, and Z-ers). These young women provide a great source of inspiration for this way of dressing. For example, mixing jeans with upscale jackets started with our daughters. Casual is what the younger generation knows best—as the following mothers and daughters so beautifully illustrate.

No Excuses

Lady looks like a dude!

Hee-Haw

Her other look must be overalls.

FOREVER COOL

Going Green

Citrus, apple, and a bit of olive harmoniously set "the green look" here. These comfortable layered outfits are basic yet full of visual energy. Daughter Ann wears the long and sheer fitted tunic, while mom Lura wears a shirt/jacket combination that provides coverage while still making for a stylish look. Judicious touches of golden yellow and white don't compete with our green statement.

The Right Stuff

Here, ethnic Bakelite jewelry in rust olive and golden yellow mixes seamlessly with a yellow summer tote and flat leather sandals.

steal this

Lura's outfit, while classic, tailored, and feminine, would add years to Ann. Ann's look is ageless and works well with her figure and spirited personality. Their sophisticated accessories can be shared.

Hippieville
Where's her protest sign?

Kitschy Accessories
This necklace will never be wearable art.

Color Cop-out
Pastel denim with red is a common (childlike) color combination mistake. Red with blue is best reserved for Old Glory.

FOREVER COOL

Cohesive Style

Feminine simplicity is the story here. Paulette and Danielle's mix-and-match outfits are comfortable, fluid, diaphanous, and, ultimately, great candidates for easy packing. Each look has an earthy, Zen feel without seeming costumey.

Local Color

The neutral palette is almost universally flattering and looks so soft with this mother and daughter's fair skin tone and light hair color. Authentic Native American turquoise jewelry adds surprise color and artful personality.

Down to Earth

The unconstructed ballet shoes pull together both outfits with the right spirit and proportion.

steal this

Mother and daughter have a similar physical look, are close in size, and share a down-to-earth personality. They can definitely wear each other's outfits and interchange these pieces, which beg to be mixed in endless ways.

Transparently Flawed

Mom Peggy's shirt is practically see-through—but not the least bit sexy. The baggy, dotted pants recall PJ bottoms and swallow up Peggy's petite shape. Should her daughters let her out of the house?

FOREVER COOL

"Boyfriend" Sexy

The fitted gray cotton knit top tucked into slightly low-rise belted chinos make the perfect pairing for Peggy. Her daughters, Stephanie and Mimi, are wearing similar looks—each a modern take on the classic, comfy chino. Totally today!

Perfect Timing

Note the big silver watch—it offers a wonderful masculine touch and sportiness that makes Peggy's look even sexier.

steal this

Go ahead, raid each other's closets! But Mom, steer clear of Mimi's basketball sneakers.

Woman Overboard!

Jeanne's gray shorts and her gray and white Hawaiian shirt look like they just washed up on shore.

Extra Freight

These clothes are boxy and too big— Jeanne has enough room to fit her daughter, Selina, inside! Jeanne's shapely legs get lost amid the amorphous billowy shorts.

Bag It

The black mark on her outfit is supposedly a purse.

FOREVER COOL

She Cleans Up Nicely!

Slim-fitting knee-length shorts and an elongated fitted shirt give Jeanne a long, lean look. The apple-green sweater can be effortlessly tossed over the shirt if it gets cold. This city-or-country style offers ample coverage and is a great alternative to short shorts.

In Living Color

Bright green and raspberry are an unexpected pairing. A high-intensity take on the classic preppy pink/green combo.

It's in the Bag

Small accents on Jeanne's straw bag draw color from both their outfits without being too matchy-matchy.

A Touch of Glitter

Gold thongs and silver flats add a bit of fun.

steal this

Mother and daughter can change outfits—but please, ladies, don't fight over the bag!

Confused Style
The pink sweater is a failed attempt at being sexy.

Saying Volumes
Her skirt looms large, adding pounds and years.

FOREVER COOL

True to Form

This story is about shirtdresses: so versatile, figure friendly, and timeless. While Abby wears her shirttail-hemmed frilled version over bare legs, mom adds white tapered pants to her simpler style, offering crisp coverage and a fresh feel.

Shaping Up

The obi sash gives Diana a waist and a sexier look than if the top were left loose, a viable option if a waistline needs defining.

Wow Factor

The feel of the brilliant silver accessories enhances the cool gray and light blue palette.

steal this

Diana should avoid the junior look of the ruffled shirtdress in favor of sophisticated simplicity. Abby can copy her mom's ageless outfit and also look terrific.

Double Trouble

Both mom and grandmother have taken fashion detours. Katherine's oversize sweater vest takes full possession of her geography.

Tight Squeeze

Daughter Nancy's purple tie-dyed T-shirt is straight from a time capsule and represents wishful thinking. Those were the days, huh?

"My mom goes for comfort, but some things are really wacky. When we tell her, she always says, 'Really? But I get so many comments about this hat, scarf, shirt,' et cetera."
—Nancy's daughter

FOREVER COOL

The Great Equalizer

Grandmom Katherine, daughter Nancy, and granddaughter Kate are wearing the same quintessentially American dark blue jean jacket. From age twenty-three to eighty-six, they all look amazing in the current cut.

Natural Women

Light makeup plus free and loosely styled hair give these women a natural look.

If the Shoe Fits

Sturdy black patent leather mocs give the matriarch of this family modern ease while still allowing for comfortable navigation. Daughter and granddaughter pull off trendier platforms, which lend them height.

steal this

Well, they each have their own jacket. Here is a perfect example of a classic piece that became so versatile as young women mixed their denim jacket with everything from shorts to dresses. They can also easily trade pants.

Sensible Overload
Diana is practical and undoubtedly comfortable . . . but is that all that really matters?

Shapeless in Seattle . . .
. . . and anywhere else this look shows up.

The Wrong Shoe
Comfy is her rule, but why not consider the perfect sandals?

FOREVER COOL #1

Share and Share Alike

Diana is sleekly modern and ageless in her simple attire. Daughter Abby's outfit conveys a similar sensibility, but her youth and figure allow for a more form-fitting top.

Cohesive Color

A neutral color palette offers endless possibilities. Pairing a dark neutral with the bright lightness of pure white ensures a fresh effect.

A Shoe-In

Ballet-style flats, whether slightly pointed or the comfy round-toed version that Mom wears, are the perfect classic sexy-casual accessory for an understated look.

steal this

The skirt, sweater, and shoes are ageless—but note that Diana's necklace has a more sophisticated look and is perfect to deflect attention from an aging neckline.

FOREVER COOL #2

Great White Way

Here's another successful take on this clean, fresh, and simple palette. Going all-white without breaking the line results in a put-together look that elongates the figure.

Expect the Unexpected

Think color . . . think texture. Here the accessories are welcome surprises, fun in proportion (oversize), materials (patent and straw), and neutral brown as well as this eye-popping orange color.

> "We both want to be Audrey Hepburn!"
> —Abby

steal this

The simplicity and classic style of the fitted sleeveless shirt and "Audrey" pants (after you-know-who) are forever. The hat may require attitude, but if you've got it, this style can be yours.

Think of casual clothing as a way of showing off terrific style with total ease.

So Dated!
This '70s outfit is enough to give you the blues.

Silly Stuff
The big denim shirt splashed with meaningless art serves no function other than to hide Judy's lovely figure.

"Senior" Addiction
Canvas sneakers will not bring back the teen years.

FOREVER COOL

Right On!
Mom celebrates her health by wearing this body-conscious classic polo. Daughter Carolyn's looser-fitting polo is perfect for her curvier shape.

Color Punch
Bright yellow and green emphasize the happy spirit of these breast cancer charity tops with graphic simplicity.

The Right Denim
Dark navy boot-cut jeans in a great fit-and-flare silhouette complete the sleek, slimming lines of mother's and daughter's outfits. (With a bit of stretch, a boon for curvy gals, they are comfortable, too!)

If the Shoe Fits
Both women wear patent leather—the most practical, fun, and long-lasting material two feet will ever enjoy.

steal this

They already have!

61

Bonding Style
Who's the grandmother here? Their outfits qualify both of them.

Identity Crisis
Could this be mom Nancy, who also wore a tie-dyed T-shirt elsewhere?

Pastel Predictable
Why do older folks think they should return to nursery colors?

"Styles have changed so much, but I still like to look my best at eighty-six, and I keep up by reading the magazines and newspapers."
—Katherine

FOREVER COOL

Balancing Act

Katherine, Kate, and Nancy are in a neutral palette that has a relaxed feel. Each woman is wearing an easy proportion for her body, shape, and height.

Well Grounded

Grandmother must wear a totally flat shoe and loves her driving moccasins. Kate and Nancy can still find the height and comfort they seek in sturdy but stellar platforms.

In the Mix

Kate wears a lariat-style necklace of pearls strung on a leather string. It's a rustic yet feminine accessory that translates well in this earthy mix of soft cottons and brown hues.

steal this

All three generations can share the palette and fabrics. The shape of each of these jackets and slacks serves to either accentuate or simply skim the figure. Young Kate is wearing the most youthful yet ageless of all three jackets. The necklace can definitely make the rounds.

Print-Out!
Is she planning a rose tattoo next?

Style Inappropriate
Minis are great for her young daughter, not Diana.

Color Bomb
Gaudy colors project a gaudy personality.

Foot Flops
High-heeled yellow shoes complete the "Hey, look at me!" getup.

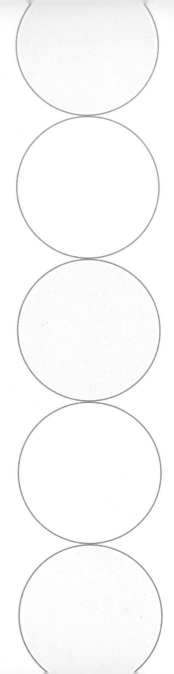

FOREVER COOL

In Living Color!

Color can be amazing. Mom Diana shares this warm summer palette with Abby. Diana wears simple blocks of color that work well for her figure and go beautifully together. Abby's delicate frame inherited her mom's beautiful broad shoulder line. The floral strapless dress highlights her shoulders and gorgeous skin.

In the Mix

Natural accessories such as Diana's red coral necklace and straw bag mix well with high-style gold sandals, which also accentuate her yellow tapered slacks. Abby's sexy platform espadrilles complement the feel and color of her sundress.

steal this

While Diana cannot borrow her daughter's dress, both generations shine with creative color done well.

Harsh Reality

No woman can seem soft with such severe color and style.

Costume Glitz

Linda's casbah look has been through a thousand and one nights.

Hair-Raising Look

Hair and makeup overkill.

"Certain styles will come back years later and can become a fashion faux pas if they're no longer age appropriate or right for your body."
—Linda's niece

FOREVER COOL

Getting Fresh

With a redo Linda looks like a breath of fresh air in a classic Moroccan tunic and pant. All-white linen provides the softness that complements her face and figure. Laura goes more island-funky with her printed Moroccan tunic paired with jeans.

Accessory Spice

Laura keeps it casual and protects her redhead's complexion with a fun, beachy hat. Her straw clutch with faux coral is in the same spirit, as are her thin-strapped sandals. Linda projects casual glam with silver/cork platform shoes and large silver hoop earrings.

steal this

All the pieces are ageless. The Moroccan tunic is an incredibly versatile, figure-friendly item that qualifies as a must-have, so be creative—mix and match.

Woodstock Come Lately
Boomer hippies need to check their calendars—it's forty years later.

Confused Style
Her hairstyle says "first grade," her skimpy lace top says "teenybopper," her patchwork ethnic skirt says "over-the-hill hippie," and her orthopedic moccasins say "ready for Geritol." Advice: make "peace" with style.

FOREVER COOL

Funky Town

The embroidery and ethnic spin is evident in Kate and Paula's dresses. Full of personality and only revealing what is beautiful on each woman, the dresses prove age appropriate, sexy, and charming at once. Paula's fluid, white, casual slacks ensure she doesn't look as if she's trying to be her daughter's age again.

Happy Feet

Only flats will do for this lighthearted, somewhat costumey, innocent bohemian look.

Get It Together

Ethnic jewelry is a chance to express individuality, and less isn't necessarily more. Worn sparingly or in stacks, it is truly a creative touch.

steal this

As alluded to earlier, Kate's dress is just right for someone her age or younger. Kate may also decide to borrow mom's long tunic and wear it beautifully as a dress. But, Paula, sit on your hands, except of course to borrow Kate's jewelry.

Anything Goes!

Well, you'd think that's the rule if a huge pink sweatshirt can be paired with a poorly fitting pair of slacks . . . and high heels.

The Big Cover-up

Why do so many women of a certain age choose to lose themselves in their clothes? Nothing is gained, except serious weight.

Seeing Pink

When glasses are pink, does the world seem rosier?

FOREVER COOL

Knit Picking

Sweater dressing fills the bill for women of any age. Warmth, layering opportunity, and welcome coverage are all part of this easy, fluid style. Mom Chris found a terrific thigh-length simple cashmere sweater, which she flung over a fresh white cotton long-sleeved T-shirt. Her boot-cut cotton velvet jeans elongate slim legs. Her daughter Cindy loves the long line her sweater coat affords her, and it allows her to feel comfortable in form-fitting, sexy, slim-legged, pegged navy jeans.

True to Form

Ballet flats are perfect for pegged pants. Mom's one-and-a-half-inch-heel brown boot is comfortable and right for her subtly flared pant.

steal this

Mom's sweater/T-shirt combo is age appropriate and youthful. But it may age Cindy a bit. Conversely Chris can wear Cindy's ageless turtleneck and long sweater—it will do her equal justice—but she needs to stick to her perfect jeans. Cindy's jeans demand a sexy figure and are more appropriate at her age.

Shorting Yourself

Paulette's skirt has everything wrong with it, but the short length is its number one eyesore. Having long, shapely legs at a certain age doesn't mean a mini is still appropriate.

Acid Dreams

Acid-washed anything should have been long gone after the '80s.

Booted Out

Surely those boots should have been thrown out with everything else.

FOREVER COOL

Sweater Sense

Sweaters are a girl's best friends. Paulette and daughter Danielle are happy in these fashionable yet classic sweaters that are so easy to toss on. The fluid sweaters are paired on both women with dark denim bootleg jeans that give a slim silhouette to balance the volume on their torsos.

Long and Short of It

Paulette's lovely legs are best served by wearing a slim jean, narrow pant, or on other occasions a skirt that hovers at about knee length.

Plum Beautiful!

Purple and navy are the basis for this creative color play. Danielle's plum sweater color is related to Paulette's bright purple hue. Almost-navy denim jeans contribute interesting harmony.

steal this

If they weren't such great friends, too, they could have a fight over these interchangeable goodies.

Thinking Old

Where do I start? How about that prefab "ladylike" knit dress and matching cardigan? Perfect . . . for nothing but a charitable donation.

Accessory to the Crime

Hedy has grabbed a bag that has no relevance in style or color to her outfit, and she compounds the awful ensemble by wearing the ladylike version of orthopedic shoes. She is guilty of ignoring form and focusing solely on function.

FOREVER COOL

Easy Does It

It doesn't take much to get this casual look together. Hedy and Mia can apply it to 85 percent of their lifestyle (including certain work days). Simply layer a sweater over a button-down, fitted shirt or T-shirt (white brightens the complexion), then step into bootleg chinos or jeans. Notice nothing is too rigid, perfect, overaccessorized, or self-conscious, which lends a youthful spirit.

Best Picks

Hedy's midnight navy carryall bag is less predictable than a black bag. Mia likewise made an unconventional choice, a moss-green bag that works with her pointy brown leather boots.

steal this

All these youthful pieces combine so simply but with great attention to form and are truly ageless. Only body type and shape (not birthday) should inform which style looks best: Hedy's longer, thinner knit sweater, or Mia's shorter, thicker knit zip-up, which is more demanding on the figure. These two gals can easily switch.

Seasonally Challenged

This look is more than chilling.
Gloria's top celebrates snowflakes,
and she seems set for the cold, but
she'll catch one with those hokey
chambray cutoffs.

No More Wire Glasses!

Her rimless glasses are not a youthful
choice, and they are, ultimately, an
aging factor on her, as they are on
most boomer-aged women who wear
them. (Sorry; rimless glasses work
only for men.)

Matchy-Matchy

That red bag and those red shoes are
bad enough, but matching them up?
Doesn't red mean "Stop"?

FOREVER COOL

They've Got the Goods

Black is practical and the color of choice for these city dwellers. Gloria's version zips up and has sweater sleeves (had the jacket been all leather, her broad upper frame would have looked too boxy). She softens her look with brown cotton velvet slacks and wears a collarless black knit top. Anything else would have choked her neckline. Sally looks modern, luxe, edgy, and sexy in her black single-breasted three-button leather sport jacket over a black turtleneck and paired with fresh white bootleg jeans (great all year 'round).

Balancing Act

Wearing black boots supplies streamlined height by extending the predominant color of the outfit down to the feet.

steal this

Except for Gloria's slacks, which are age (and size) appropriate for her, these clothes are basically, once again, ageless. The reason? The motorcycle jacket and hunt-style sport jacket are classics, as are the jeans.

Denim Disaster

This cutesy denim outfit is mismatched, ill fitting, and embellished to be artsy but simply looks silly.

Color Catastrophe

Portia attempts to color coordinate, but she's working with a terribly loud and unsophisticated palette.

Accessory Adversity

Her clashing tote further emphasizes the poor color and print choices she's made.

FOREVER COOL

The Simple Life

Portia and Paige are ready for a fall day together. Layering clothing comprised of neutral colors allows them to create not only these two outfits, but also numerous other mix-and-match versions. Here texture adds interest, while simplicity lends a look of uncontrived ease.

Surprise Factor

When using an understated palette with only solids, adding those leopard-print ballet flats gives Portia's outfit a bit of unexpected glamour.

Fresh Faced

The natural look that mom and daughter share actually dwindles the appearance of years between them.

steal this

Mom wears an outfit that is classic at the core, and the cut is adjusted to be slightly conservative to fit her figure and age. Paige wears an outfit that, in concept, Portia could wear, but this particular cut makes it work better on Paige's figure. As usual, interchangeable accessories are a bonding force.

Taking Her Lumps

Yesterday's cowl-neck tunic and bulky sweater with oversize buttons and too-long skirt are taxing for this small woman's frame to carry. Poor-quality materials and color choices contribute to the cheap and tired look.

Accessories After the Fact

The shoes and the bags are the wrong scale and color, and they look as if they were chosen for another outfit.

"I actually thought my mom always looked great when I was growing up. It's ironic that I find she has a harder time as she's gotten older."
—Chris's daughter

FOREVER COOL

Smooth Transition

Mom Chris has entrusted daughter Cindy with the finishing touches on her natural makeup look. Chris looks light on her feet and unified in her monochromatic outfit, as does Cindy.

Director's Cut

The unbroken long lines of these coats skim their bodies and give the illusion of height. Cindy's figure allows her to wear a more fitted version, while a looser, body-skimming fit better serves Chris. Cindy's neckline looks good in a turtleneck, and Chris, whose neck is shorter and wider, is flattered by an open neckline.

steal this

Chris can wear the bootleg-style pants that her daughter is wearing, but Cindy would not achieve a sexy look from her mom's ever so slightly pegged slacks. While ladies of all ages may want greater height, Chris's shoes are super comfortable (that thick rubber sole!) and right for her style of slacks; Cindy's high-heeled, pointy-toed boots may get more use in her closet (sorry, Mom!).

The Farmer in the Dell
Is Yasue visiting that little house on the prairie? A shining example of how an outfit can detract from a pretty face.

Out of Proportion
Whether you're tall or short, long denim skirts for anytime are a no-no.

Black Out
Black accessories do not make a corny outfit hip.

"I was a very well-dressed child. Completely put together from head to toe . . . except for the time my mother sent me to preschool without underwear. Oops!"
—Yasue's daughter

FOREVER COOL

Under Wraps

Send these women a congratulatory cable—knit, that is! Sweater layering, again, can be an imaginative way to stay warm and fashionable. Shawls and capelets provide texture and attitude.

Well Heeled

Both mother Yasue and daughter Michelle are petite and enjoy the lift their respective shoes give them. The bootleg jean is the best jean to wear with any sort of heel.

Purrrfect Print

Including the leopard bag adds excitement and practicality to Yasue's stylish outfit—it's an easy tote that does not encumber her shoulders.

steal this

Yasue could wear Michelle's outfit because she is so petite and in great shape. Michelle is still too young to carry off the sophistication of Yasue's one-piece sweater-shawl combo.

They Shoot Horses . . . Don't They?

Put this look out of its misery! Demonstrating sensibility without style sense might be comfortable, but Paulette has never explored her options.

Seeing Red

A bland color combination that is bad in all ways is punctuated by an unfortunately positioned red fanny pack that all eyes will center on.

FOREVER COOL

Fresh Pick

A ripe take on preppy, mother Paulette has been nudged well by slightly mod daughter Danielle. Preppy style was around in Paulette's youth, but it took Danielle to create a fresh take for her look today and inspire her mom to consider this classic, ageless, and highly mixable style for herself.

Color Connection

Mother and daughter both make the most of green—Paulette's cashmere turtleneck is a bright and unpredictable olive, while Danielle's edgy argyle is composed of a sophisticated charcoal gray, off white, and a lighter version of olive. The simplicity of their outfits is accentuated by color blocking, and Paulette's outfit conjures country style, while Danielle's look is definitely downtown.

steal this

Danielle can wear Mom's look, but Paulette may be pushing the envelope in her daughter's gear.

The Snore Factor

Boring clothes lead to a dull outcome.
No thought was given to color or
more youthful choices.

And If That's Not Enough . . .

Her jeans are too short, her exposed
socks are too white, and her wrong
accessories induce snoring. Zzzzz . . .

FOREVER COOL

She's Alive!

And ready for anything in her military-inspired coral blazer. Both mother Judy and daughter Carolyn are wearing a canvas of dark clothing punctuated by vibrant color. Picking and choosing color strategy is part and parcel of the art of the mix.

Fit for Service

Both ladies wear form-fitting, body-skimming styles that enhance shape and gloss over flaws.

Sure-Footed

Short boots and low heels might work equally well, but flats give these gals a sporty ease that playfully supports the happy spirit of their outfits.

steal this

These outfits are ageless, depending on figure. Judy's double-breasted jacket, for example, enhances her slim silhouette. However, Carolyn is best served by a more loosely fitting eggplant topper. They'll have a tough time deciding who gets the bag.

Run Afoul
Stealing from a husband's or son's closet does not make a winning goal.

Packing It On
Layering clothes without thought for color or fit results in a sloppy, overstuffed appearance.

FOREVER COOL

Thumbs Up!

These ladies are playing a winning game in these outfits. Portia is comfortable and stylish in a sweater reminiscent of the classic toggle coat. Paige is wearing a fitted, quilted all-weather jacket that can be worn on its own or layered with either a down vest or a heavier jacket.

Confident Color

Again, neutrals are so easy to work with and build on—and are rarely wrong.

steal this

Both ladies enjoy bootleg jeans for their length-giving cut and comfort. The ageless sweater Portia wears requires height, while the ultra-classic jacket petite Paige models would work on any woman.

Arrested Development

Dressing like a teenybopper only makes her look more like her grandmother. This "conversation heart" sweatshirt is too saccharine for words.

Lock It Up

The senior sensible red shoes and bag don't rehabilitate this delinquent look.

> Cindy still looks into my eyes to read how she looks. If I seem to disapprove, she either responds with, 'Yeah, I wasn't sure,' and changes, or tells me, 'You have to get with it!' I may be behind the times, but it still makes me feel special knowing my opinion means something to her."
> —Chris

FOREVER COOL

No Fuss, No Muss

Chris gets a kiss for keeping in stylish step with her daughter, Cindy. Basic gym togs inspire both women's easy looks. However, using high-end fabrics such as fine cotton knits, velour, and cashmere upgrades the personality and versatility of their outfits. Whether shopping or traveling, these looks are practical and packable.

True to Form

By not wearing the obvious choice—sneakers—mother and daughter look more put together and feminine in their ultracasual looks.

steal this

Chris is wearing a top that's modest, while Cindy can get away with a more revealing and slim-fitting cardigan. They can steal each other's color palette and that adorable bag.

Fashion Freezes Over

She may be nice and cozy, but she's cold on style.

Worst Picks

A bit of this and that, all bundled up and simplistically tied into a bad blend of color, fabric, and amorphous shape.

"I was always of the opinion that to look good in clothes you had to have a lot of money. But I now know that although money is a component, knowing how to fit your body and what your strengths and limitations are in wearing certain styles, cuts, and colors are even more important."
—Gloria

FOREVER COOL

In the Trenches

The classic trench coat has many stylish derivatives, as seen here in just two examples on mom Gloria and daughter Sally. Neutral-toned coats provide warmth and coverage, whether the ladies are wearing jeans or skirts.

A Touch of Color

Gloria's beautiful scarf works well with her coloring and adds interest to her outfit. Note it is tied in an unself-conscious but artful way.

steal this

Though Sally's nylon coat is more youthful and sporty, there is no age requirement for either coat. Sally wears her jeans with a pointy flat that may be less comfortable for Gloria. The scarf, from a high-end fashion house famous for its silk scarves, will be a family heirloom coveted by all generations.

Disappearing Act

Looking so conservative and uninspired, Peggy is guaranteed to go unnoticed. Simplicity works when it has a mix of texture, quality fabric, and perhaps vibrant color play or interesting proportion. This outfit is simply bland.

Sensible Overload

So utilitarian is her outfit, it conjures a uniform.

FOREVER COOL

Singing in the Rain

Rainy weather needn't dampen great style. Peggy's black patent topper is a great alternative to waterproof or rubberized fabrics. Her daughters—Mimi, in a lightweight, longer safari-style jacket, and Stephanie, in her short tent topper—are equally set, rain or shine. Long-legged and ultraslim Mimi wears white straight-leg jeans, while her mom and sister wear the elongating bootleg versions.

Under One Umbrella

Invest in a fun umbrella (and try not to lose it!). All three outfits benefit from the extra punch this leopard-print version (great with all neutral-colored outfits) provides.

steal this

These jacket styles are interchangeable. Even great-grandmother can experiment with all of them. Their jeans are right on all ages, allowing for their heights and proportions, as are their shoes. Stephanie chose the patent platforms, which bring her closer in height with Peggy, in her one-and-a-half-inch heel boots, and Mimi, in her patent ballet flats.

Uninspired Style
Predictable and safe, this look inspires only winter blahs.

Cheap Stuff
That fake-fur-lined vest leaves its origin to the imagination.

FOREVER COOL

The Best and the Brightest

Bright color in the cold season can pump up the mood when it's so needed and enliven a winter pallor. Judy and Carolyn embrace the season with layers that can be added to or easily shed. Using royal blue, coral red, touches of grass green, and gray and dark denim to give the eye a rest . . . it all works.

Super Natural

That's the look. An un-made-up look is the only way this youthful outdoors style realizes its true beauty.

steal this

Share and share alike is this mother and daughter's motto. Note that Carolyn can wear only slim, straight ("skinny") jeans in order to get that smooth look in her rubber boots. On other days she looks best in bootlegs. Because Judy is ultrathin she can wear slim-style jeans over her low-heeled black patent boots, or the bootleg ones she models here.

Bingo Time
Would a younger person ever buy this look?

Old-Age Coloring Book
Teal (big in the '80s) is part of the "senior" pack of crayon colors.

FOREVER COOL

Urban Dwellers

The citified version of the sleeveless-down-vest look is, of course, all black. So easy, versatile, and practical, this way of dressing can span all sorts of activities. Interchange the components with other neutral colors (e.g., a charcoal or brown turtleneck on Sally), and multiple outfits manifest effortlessly.

Focal Point

A big sporty silver watch would look great with Sally's outfit, but her orange-banded timepiece adds a playful and unexpected touch. Likewise, Gloria's watch also catches one's attention with its orange face.

steal this

The classic down vest look is what they can absolutely share. The particular cuts of their actual clothing are right for their respective figures. The stylish yet comfortable walking shoe styles are options for mom or daughter, as are those youthful watches.

Linebacker Looks
Mistakes are only good if we learn from them.

Odd Coupling
How strange that such a conservative outfit is topped by an extreme vestige of the '80s—shoulder pads.

FOREVER COOL

Just My Luxe

Magnificent red hair is not all this mom and daughter share. Loosely fitting jackets, one a short cashmere sweater and the other longer and in wool-cashmere, are casual layers over wool-cashmere turtlenecks. Mom Ellen is feeling luxurious in her bootleg brown suede slacks, which add texture to her monochrome outfit. Her short two-and-a-half-inch-heel boots lend just the height she needs. Daughter Mariana arrives at a more casual look with jeans and snow boots.

steal this

Eventually Mariana will be of the age to look great in Ellen's classic and sophisticated pieces. However, Mariana, be generous to your mom, because she can easily wear your look today.

chapter three
work it out

Work has become a minefield of style faux pas for boomer women who want to be comfortable and feminine while still looking professional and modern. There are so many ways to slip up (supershort skirts, too-revealing tops, et cetera) or get stuck in a rut (red-jacket-and-black-skirt "power suits" left over from the 1980s, or the oh-so-ubiquitous and predictable silky knits by a Chanel-wannabe maker). What you can appropriately wear has much to do with your office's formality—or lack of it. Corporate offices often require women (and men) to project a look of trustworthiness and intelligence. But in trying to maintain the propriety called for in such surroundings, you may find yourself trapped in a boring "ladylike" interpretation of a man's suit. A more relaxed office also presents challenges—how far can you go? The casualness that younger colleagues might get away with could leave you with a pink slip—and I'm not talking about lingerie! Whatever you wear, it must be suitable and contemporary, without landing you in a sexual sphere or being so laid-back as to minimize your professionalism. When you look in the mirror you should feel confident that your clothes enhance the skills you offer, not distract from or downplay them. After all, you could be up for the same job as your daughter—or working right next to her in the same office!

No Flair Apparent

Could Allyson be any safer? Even if her job calls for a conservative image, she looks dowdy, thanks to the utterly predictable suit and the length of her skirt.

Staid Accessories

Gold clip earrings and matching gold necklace, sensible shoes, and the bag are innocuous, adding no modern or stylish flair to her already boring outfit.

FOREVER COOL #1

Work Force

Allyson and daughter Catherine are ready for action. For any workday except the most formal, this jacket-and-pants outfit is perfect. The jackets can be worn closed if more formality is called for. The youthful spirit of the classic safari jacket, its neutral olive color, and the fresh white tank top beneath paired with simple slacks give both women an ageless persona.

Perfect Package

Allyson's bag can fit business papers and picks up on her safari style with its reptile detail. Catherine's fun sport watch adds vitality to her comfortable look. Her brown leather platforms help create a long, lean effect.

steal this

As you can see both ladies can employ this look fully. Safari jackets come in traditional styling or with fashion-inspired twists as modeled here. All generations can partake in wearing them with slacks, or knee-length skirts if over forty, and even shorter skirts for the younger set. Mom's bag is too big for Catherine, but she can easily find one that suits, because her simple look and palette is so easy to accessorize.

FOREVER COOL #2

Pencil Me In

This simple outfit comprised of a fitted turtleneck and bootleg slacks is bound to make the most of these two slim-figured women. The neutral, almost monochrome, effect of the gray color play gives them a fluid silhouette. This classic ensemble has dozens of mix-match possibilities and works well for most jobs (or just for dress-down Fridays).

In the Loop

Their accessories have a consistent circle motif, in both the earrings and Allyson's belt. The large (but still sane) circumference of all the loops makes their look even more hip.

steal this

Ready, get set, go for it! Both mom and daughter can share the style as long as it fits. Only caveat: Mom must size down one notch on her earrings, as she does here, as opposed to Catherine's larger pair, and Allyson's belt is too overwhelming for Catherine (smaller hoops would work better).

Whatever you wear must be suitable and contemporary without landing you in a saucy sphere.

Time Capsule
Yes, we humans did wear this look once . . . long ago.

Schoolmarm Effect
So buttoned-up Houdini could not hasten her departure from this conservative cage.

"I'm always trying to keep up with new styles (think belly shirts of the '90s or the sky-high heels I have come to love) that often don't complement my mom's sense of propriety."
—Yasue's daughter

FOREVER COOL

Fast Forward

Modern times have transformed today's mother and professional woman, Yasue. Her daughter, Michelle, loves her mother's hip sense of style now. A bit edgy yet feminine, they look appropriate for their ages and work. These black-and-white outfits are minimalist and fresh.

steal this

The color scheme is universally hip. However, Yasue is wearing a more sophisticated version of the theme (an off-white scoop-neck sweater and knee-length black leather skirt). Michelle's junior version exposes more arm and leg, and is still okay at her young age. Both ladies share the black opaque hose that streamline their legs. They are the same shoe size, so only the heel height may make a difference for comfort.

Unsuit-able Style

Even Ellen's grandmother would nix her ladylike and matronly jacket. With no thought to proportion, those too-long, pegged slacks slouch and gather in a puddle at her ankles. Those high-heeled pumps give her feet a pedestal effect (a popular, but extremely unfortunate, 1980s look).

Insult to Injury

You know she wears that bag with all her outfits. The gobs of gold costume jewelry could sink a ship—as they do her look.

> "I have learned from my mom that it is important to have a presence at all times. Clothes are an individual's communication tools, she says. That is what determines how people will respond to you."
> —Ellen's daughter

FOREVER COOL

Cream of the Cropped

The cropped jacket is loosely fitted and flatters most figures without the demands more constructed styles impose. Ellen's coloring is enhanced by the bright red-orange hue, highlighted by the simple black "Audrey" ankle-length slacks, black turtleneck, and almost flat kitten-heel pumps (so '50s!) that provide perfect proportion. Mariana's smile has as much to do with her gorgeous crinkled leather brown jacket as with her similar slacks (which expose her lovely ankles) and ballet flats.

Expect the Unexpected

It's part of great style to mix in a surprise color, texture, print, or other element. Here the dark green patent bag works with either outfit and is more interesting than a black bag would be.

steal this

We really have a cross-gen grab bag here. It's all very youthful yet ageless. The only caveat for Mom at work is that her ankle-length pant must truly be at her ankle (as Ellen's are). This mother and daughter better plan ahead for first dibs.

Failing Grade
This principal will never get an apple for style.

A Common Problem
How many times have you seen this frumpy floral skirt and heavy wool blazer/turtleneck combo coming and going in school hallways, banks, insurance companies, and a host of other offices?

Time-Out
These sorry accessories need a recess.

FOREVER COOL

E for Excellence

Mom Susan wears a beautiful silver-gray suit in an all-season fabric, while daughter Alexis wears a gray wool turtleneck with a twist—short sleeves. She pairs it with a wool tweed pencil skirt.

Gorgeous Gray

A softer alternative to black, gray is universally flattering (just pick the right shade) and sophisticated. It allows for flexibility in mixing and matching with other neutrals (think white, black, brown, tan, camel, beige, cream).

Pulled Together

Classically oriented accessories with touches of silver set off the gray outfits.

steal this

The pantsuit and the skirt-and-sweater look have stood the test of time. Here they are fresh in a current cut. Mother and daughter could steal each other's outfits and accessories, allowing for fit.

A Bad Angle

Often presented as fashionably edgy, garments that substitute endless hem variations for a true hemline simply confuse the eye.

Harsh Reality

Hard clothes conjure up hard times. The flawed mixing of shades, the fabrics, the proportions, and the tacky accessories are anything but easy on the eyes.

"Laura is quite the style mogul who has no problem burning a hole in her pocket on any up-and-coming fashion—she has no shame!"
—Linda

FOREVER COOL

And the Winner Is . . .

Knits! These looks provide age-appropriate softness to Aunt Linda and like-a-daughter niece Laura. Wearing knits that skim her shape without clinging, and neutral colors that don't complicate her small frame shows off Linda's adorable figure. Laura's more lively and colorful dress flatters her figure, and with her height, she can carry a bold pattern.

If the Shoe Fits

Each woman's outfit is complemented by a suitable boot—Linda gains height and sleekness from her shiny, dark brown, knee-high boot, which meets her skirt without a gap; Laura's Native American–inspired boots give her outfit a fun spin rather than a sexual one—perfect for her job as a boutique sales manager.

steal this

Knits run the gamut, and these two looks are appropriate for their wearers' respective ages. No sharing in this case.

Do I Know You?

Say good-bye to this dreary parochial school uniform look.

Past Imperfect

Pieces that are dated, badly cut, and ill proportioned have worn out their welcome.

FOREVER COOL

Simple Perfection

Hedy and daughter-in-law Mia are best friends with a shared love of simplicity. Again, gray is the color of choice because of its obvious polish and professionalism. Great cuts and beautiful fabrics do these classic clothes justice. The ability to accessorize and change the look and function of these pieces is endless.

steal this

This happy pair could interchange their looks, right down to the brown-toned shoes, bag, and bold watches.

All Wrong

When good color happens to bad outfits—gray is great, except when it's on ill-fitting clothes. The bow is the finishing touch on a badly wrapped package.

FOREVER COOL

Crisp Connection

Ifé and Nicole are mother and daughter in spirit—two women could not be closer, especially in their easy and versatile shirt-and-pant look. The beauty of a fresh white shirt is that it can be worn in so many ways and still look professional. Nicole's look is trendier; note how the bottom of the shirt and long sleeves extend beyond the black cashmere tee. Ifé's tailored shirt (because it is vulnerable white, she has quite a few) skims her body and complements her shape. Her black cashmere cardigan hangs languidly over her shoulders for interest and warmth.

Exclamation Point

The turquoise bag with silver accents lends the wow factor to an otherwise two-color combo.

steal this

Basically they are wearing the same outfit, but in cuts and styles that suit them. Think of the white shirt as a wardrobe staple no matter your age. In gathering all these simple pieces both generations are establishing an easy core for the art of the mix.

Goody-goody

So eager to please, she will be perceived otherwise. Her cutesy-meets-matronly outfit totally lacks allure.

FOREVER COOL

Great Call

Mother Paula and daughter Kate both made good choices when they picked out similar double-breasted sweater jackets. They look professional yet feminine. No rigid looks here. Tall, slim Kate can easily don a pleated skirt with a bold pattern, while her mom looks best in straightforward charcoal-gray slacks.

Expect the Unexpected

Using cream-colored shoes with black details is much more fun than safe black choices would have been.

steal this

These clothes are similar in feeling and share the double-breasted style, but each woman's outfit is appropriately interpreted for her age and figure.

You should feel confident that your clothes enhance the skills you offer.

Where's the Fire?

Look out! This '80s stiff, red suede suit is alarmingly loud. The accessories only fan the flames.

Vision Problems

Cynthia's wire glasses are aging, plain and simple.

FOREVER COOL

Walking Softly

Though mom Cynthia and daughter Malene both mean business, they accomplish it by wearing soft looks that enhance their figures through gently draping, fluid fabrics.

Color Craft

Both ladies wear a gradation of shades, from true black, as in Cynthia's pegged pants, to the charcoal gray of Malene's dress, to the palest gray of Cynthia's suede flats. For added spark, Malene's oxblood shoes (as opposed to an obvious pure red) and Cynthia's red and silver earrings fill the bill.

20/20 Vision

Choosing a contemporary frame that says "I'm wearing glasses and proud of it" is a much more youthful approach.

steal this

Malene's ageless dress is also appropriate for Cynthia but would make certain demands on her figure. However, Malene's youth and hourglass figure wouldn't be as well served by the sophisticated and comfortable yet not so body-conscious look that works for her mom.

Too Much Information

Surely those clothes are glued to her body. Nothing is left to her coworkers' imaginations.

Bling Fling

Her motto is "The more the merrier." This worthless collection of garish accessories and fakery is part of a look that begs for attention.

"Menopause granted me a very different body than the one that used to wear size-four jeans. Soft, easy fabric is now so much more important—hot flashes are much worse in scratchy, bulky clothing. Layers are my friend."
—Paula

FOREVER COOL

Intelligent Instinct

A savvy selection of neutral knits, slightly bootleg pants, and white stretch tanks gives mom Paula and daughter Kate a look their colleagues will respect. Somewhat casual (and perhaps perfect for certain professions' dressed-down Fridays), this look affords both women flexibility, mobility, and credibility.

Accent on Accessories

Great glasses, fun hoops, statement watches, short-heeled boots, and one terrific tote to carry the day's supplies—give these ladies a promotion!

steal this

Kate's long sweater/pant ensemble is a young look that would still be right for someone older if she had a figure like Kate's. Paula's outfit befits her shape and is perfect for her age; Kate has a few years to go before she should borrow it.

Take It or Leave It

Leave it. Paulette's look was never in style.

"People always mistake me for being younger. It didn't help that I used to wear glitter or T-shirts with cutesy cartoon characters. Now I aim for a more mature look and people take me more seriously."
—Paulette's daughter

FOREVER COOL

Modern Masters

Being "of today" is priceless, especially at work. Here mom and daughter realize the impact of their minimalist, sleek looks. Mom Paulette is ready for the executive suite in her hip yet feminine suit, tall suede boots, classic black pearls, and patent attaché. Daughter Danielle meets deadlines with ease in a gray scoop-neck sweater, pegged "Audrey" subtle plaid slacks, and burgundy patent ballet flats.

steal this

By all means, trade up.

No Animals Were Harmed . . .

. . . in the making of this jacket, but people were! Bad color, fabric, and form result in dysfunctional style.

FOREVER COOL

Textural Teamwork

Tortoiseshell, suede, cashmere knit, wool, linen, cane, and silver provide a collage of rich textures. Beautifully exhibited in limited colors—just brown, black, and tan—Portia and Paige's outfits will definitely be noticed and win rave reviews.

Extraordinary Accessories

Extra performance credit should be given to the tortoise chain necklace and the standout multiseason linen-and-cane bag with silver chain accent.

steal this

Mother and daughter are already sharing the skirt, which is a timeless piece for all ages. Mom should also own a basic black turtleneck, a wardrobe staple Paige enjoys. Their respective suede jackets are right for their figures, as are the boots. Paige is too young and too petite to wear the necklace, but that bag . . . better buy a duplicate.

Ladylike Layers

It's hard to warm up to this vision. So prissy and utterly conservative, the coat is reminiscent of those ubiquitous and matronly knit suits.

Dead Wrong

Susan thought she was being stylish when she bought that unfortunate dyed-fur neck warmer.

FOREVER COOL

Warming Trend

The coat you wear going to and from work is no less important than the outfit beneath. After all, who knows which power broker will be in the elevator? Susan's beautifully designed black wool coat, paired with a black turtleneck and pointy leather one-and-a-half-inch-heel boots are worn with light wool slacks but can also be worn chicly with knee-length skirts. Alexis's big blue eyes are emphasized by her robin's-egg-blue peacoat-style wool jacket. The specialty color limits her ability to wear it as her only jacket, but with black (as shown) or midnight navy, she is assured a most striking outfit.

It's Your Bag

A black bag with multiple pockets and zippers is one savvy way to be organized on a daily basis.

steal this

A perfect example of ageless outerwear and simplicity beneath it, these looks can be indulged in by both Alexis and her mom—no age requirement.

chapter four
fancy that!

We all go to dinner, attend the theater and concerts, and drop in on cocktail parties. Part of the fun and anticipation of a more formal or festive look is in the distinction it makes between ordinary, everyday life and more celebratory moments. In these cases, clothes really help transport us. Yet as we rush around trying to meet deadlines and check off our to-do lists, the joy we used to take in dressing up seems to be gone. Opting for the easier route, we allow casual style to spill over to times when some upscale chic is called for. Yes, it's true we've all gotten that sinking feeling after making the effort and then ending up sitting next to someone in jeans and a sweatshirt—and the icing, a backward baseball cap. But don't let other people's choices influence your resolve to up the ante for certain circumstances. While it's tempting to feel we can get away with looking very casual all the time, dressing up (and doing it well) for certain occasions is one way of demonstrating our regard for others and for ourselves—and our daughters, of course. Thankfully, their dress-up looks offer a youthful and modern perspective that reminds us that we don't need to stick to old rules and matronly duds. We can let loose in terms of imaginative color, texture, and line. Hey, it can be easy to bid good-bye to those staid outfits and over-the-top getups. Don't believe it? Turn the page.

Halloween Style

Pumpkin outfits are only cool at a costume party on October 31. The colors alone are a scary trick, but the jewelry can't possibly be intended as a treat.

Too Much, Too Little

So much fabric in all the wrong places. She wears an unnecessarily voluminous top but leaves herself uncovered where a bit of extra fabric would be more flattering.

FOREVER COOL

Color Me "Amazing"!

This style's success is in truly authentic use of fabric, as in Lura's easy jacket and Ann's painterly top with its brilliant hues, comfortable fabric, and simple style. Notice the prints are balanced on both ladies by white slacks.

Natural Selection

Small straw and wicker woven bags reinforce the casual dressiness of these looks. Ann's orange leather and silver cuff bracelet offers punch. Lura wears a silver cuff and earrings with an ethnic flavor that complement her lovely silver hair. The brown platforms on Ann add length, which wide pant legs require. Lura is happiest in totally flat sandals that are in keeping with her outfit's ethnic bent.

steal this

Ann's outfit is right for her figure and her age. She may be able to wear it appropriately for years to come, and Ann's daughter could certainly borrow it. However, Lura's figure and age are well served by the lines of her outfit, and the style is a bit mature for Ann.

137

Where's the Corsage?

The custom and the dress are a vestige of high school proms past. The bad news: this dress must be left over from her big night. The good news? It still fits.

FOREVER COOL

Hot Stuff!

Jeanne and Selina have got the moves, and their outfits inspire them to strut their stuff on the dance floor. Selina gets going in her yellow cashmere T-shirt paired with cotton jean-style pants in a colorful print by a design house legendary for its beautiful prints. Mom Jeanne is following her lead by wearing the same tee in black, paired with a slim palazzo pant that also boasts an amazing print from the same design house.

Weights and Balances

Both outfits take a starring role, so adding only earrings and nothing else leaves these two ladies both chic and unencumbered.

steal this

Jeanne's fluid pant style is more forgiving, but Selina can certainly borrow them next time she hits the dance floor. Selina's style requires a young demeanor and a slim figure. The T-shirts are perfect for any woman who enjoys a stylish basic (and who wouldn't?).

Prissy Missy

Going "no frills" may be a good thing sometimes. This flower-print ankle-length skirt doesn't fly today either; it only confirms her ultraconservative reservations.

Detail Disconnect

These accessories don't relate to one another.

FOREVER COOL

Prints Charming

Alexis loves to share her style secrets with her mom, Susan. It looks like the exchange goes both ways. Here simple tops, one a cotton tee, the other a sleeveless sweater set, are paired with gathered cotton skirts that have fun '50s and '60s modern-inspired motifs.

Style Inheritance

Alexis carries a vintage-style straw bag that looks adorable with her outfit. One day she will inherit Susan's Nantucket bag (usually passed from generation to generation), an iconic piece made of tightly woven rattan, topped with a magnificent carving (this one of a whale) in scrimshaw on whalebone. In keeping with tradition, her initials are engraved under the lid.

steal this

Alexis will have to wait for her bag, but other than the different (and age-appropriate) skirt lengths, these outfits work well for mother and daughter, especially since Susan's arms have maintained their tone.

Animal House

This overindulged print gives her too much square footage.

Doily Duds

This sweater could decorate her couch!

"Mum always struggled with me, as I wouldn't wear anything feminine (frilly stuff) as a young girl, and even today as an adult—but I do want to be a woman who feels confident and sexy in what I wear."
—Gloria's daughter

FOREVER COOL

The Evening Standard

The standard is high with Sally and mom Gloria modeling the classic look of the little black dress. Gloria's version flatters and covers all the right places. Sally stands proud (as she should) in her more revealing and sexy—yet also appropriate and still refined—style.

Basic Instinct

Though the black dress leaves an open invitation to accessorize to the nines, these ladies have taken the always beautiful, ever tasteful, classic minimalist approach. Pearl earrings, simple clutches, an ebony bangle, and modern three-inch pointy heels make the look.

steal this

Gloria is wearing the cut that's suitable for her age, as is Sally. But you know they will never lack for perfect accessories.

Did I Forget Something?
A sense of style, perhaps?

Pathetic Prints
This print is a garden variety of unattractive florals.

Still Expecting?
Doubtful, but the look suggests about nine months.

Anything Goes
The accessories are bad enough alone, but they definitely don't work together.

FOREVER COOL

Dancing in the Breeze

Ann and Lura are perfect dance partners. Keeping in step, Ann pairs a Moroccan-inspired green velvet tunic featuring burnished gold thread and beaded embroidery with pegged cotton pants made exciting by a bold palm leaf pattern. Lura is easily in rhythm wearing a fitted caftan in a gardenlike printed chiffon. Lura's straightforward white linen pants provide perfect balance.

A Shining Example

A bit of gold, a bit of silver. The accessories glimmer but don't detract from the wow effect of the outfits in themselves.

steal this

Ann's tunic, in the right size, would suit Lura and would optimally be paired with her own white slacks. Lura's outfit is not as youthful as Ann could still wear.

Moda Aloha
Hawaii is beautiful, but wearing it isn't.

So-Sensible Accessories
True, the bag is waterproof . . . and those sandals are comfy . . . but what happened to "attractive"?

"My mother represents integrity and a nonwasteful ethic. I think she would rather acquire a few great pieces and mix them rather than have a closet full of throwaways."
—Peggy's daughter

FOREVER COOL

Frock Stars

Peggy leads her girls by example with feminine dress. Her wrap dress shows off her slim shape and subtle curves, but also covers appropriately. Mimi and Stephanie can expose more skin but still manage to look alluring and refined.

Beauty of Brown

Each dress, in print or solid, uses brown as its pervasive color. Brown is a great neutral alternative to black and allows for imaginative accessorizing.

steal this

It may be obvious, but just in case . . . each woman is truly wearing the most appropriate dress for her age. The accessories can be rotated but not necessarily with these dresses.

No Fringe Benefits

Jeanne thinks the more fringe and moving parts, the better.

Bad Hair Day

Flat and unbecoming, her hairstyle needs reassessing and resuscitating.

Insult to Injury

Those accessories!

"My daughter, Selina, looks good in everything. It has always been a challenge to measure up to her stylish expectations."
—Jeanne

FOREVER COOL

Preppy Glamour

Upticking from an ordinary jean look is as easy as choosing to pair dark denim bootleg jeans with fun double-breasted, cropped knit jackets. Jeanne picked a navy–off-white horizontal striped version, and Selina went for the cheerful bright orange.

Totally Charming

Selina wears patent for great shine and fresh appeal. Her flower pin, gold zippered satchel, and high-heeled shoes coordinate beautifully with her gold chain belt and charm bracelet— a whimsical nod to Chanel. Jeanne changed her hairstyle and revealed a lovely face by simply wearing a black patent headband. Pearl earrings, a stack of colorful bracelets, a structured small straw tote, and patent kitten heels complete her look.

> **steal this**
>
> Winner takes all! Both women can exchange freely.

Untrue to Form

Ifé is swimming (and are those slacks dripping and pooling?) in her clothes.

Come Out, Come Out, Wherever You Are!

In clothes that serve only to cover and hide, she looks disheveled and sloppy.

FOREVER COOL

How Sweet It Is . . .

. . . when it's right. Ifé and Nicole have their cake (and eat it, too!) while wearing a favorite look in black and white. Here, Ifé is wearing a body-skimming white tank that's a bit shorter than her fluid and sheer linen sweater. She pairs them with soft black silk slacks. Nicole wears a classic and very fitted white linen jacket, paired with black, wide bootleg pants.

steal this

Ifé's outfit would not do justice to Nicole's slim body. Ifé needs an unstructured look to look her best.

Of course you can have your cake and eat it—comfortably, and appropriately, too!

Say Good Night, Gracie!
You must be exhausted by this tired look, dear readers.

In Mauve I Trust
It's the color of the senior community flag.

"Clothing does make a difference—not just in the way I look, but more important, in the way I feel about myself."
—Lura's daughter

FOREVER COOL

Ethnic Pride

Ann's dress suggests an African print, and her sheer silk and cashmere shawl is embroidered with a complementary motif. Lura's luxuriously embroidered shawl qualifies as wearable art. Colorful and imaginatively decorated with sequins and beads (also with some African motifs), this sheer shawl has such visual impact that it makes her outfit.

Accessory Smarts

Ann wears a gold sandal that plays off the yellow and burnished golden shades in her dress. Lura's bag has an intricate, tight sequined design in low-key color that bolsters rather than competes with her gorgeous shawl. She wears bronze flats for comfort but certainly hasn't sacrificed style.

steal this

The outfits are solely right for each woman's age and figure. Ann is comfortable enough physically and within her personality to share Lura's accessories (for other ensembles), especially these shawls, which require attitude to wear.

You Are So Busted!

Males may go *sniff, sniff,* as this look attracts attention . . . but never the right kind.

Eighties Redux

It was her high point and she can't let go of those days . . . and the clothes.

FOREVER COOL

Flash of Brilliance

A play on midnight navy with a bit of shine adds up to a brilliant look. Ellen is youthful in her navy scoop neck with a sweet bow appliqué, paired with dark bell-bottom jeans. Mariana holds her near and dear . . . in life and in style as well. She wears a scoop-neck navy sequin top with the same style jeans.

All That Glitters

Both bags, in different grays, have enough shine to further add to the playful glamour without overpowering it. The unusual and lovely glasslike necklace and bracelet also add dimension without fighting for visual impact.

steal this

Ellen looks best in her understated, stylish sweater, and young Mariana (given her un-made-up look) can absorb the showi-ness of her top. Both women enjoy and feel comfortable in the high heels (covered as they should be by flared bottoms) their looks warrant.

Hammock Around the Neck Syndrome

Mon Dieu! This is not what those French ladies had in mind.

So Dated

We don't need the receipt to know in what decade this outfit was purchased.

Dullness, Inc.

Burgundy, gray, and black are a grim combination.

"My mother often misses the subtleties that make an item so appealing and goes for a cheaper brand that doesn't have the same cut or fabric—and the end result just doesn't compare."
—Jeanne's daughter

FOREVER COOL

Color Wise

Great affection and a super color sense are only part of what Selina shares with her mom, Jeanne. Taking a creative risk with color and pattern makes otherwise simple outfits amazing standouts. Using a concise palette of shades of orange, brown, and green with white and tan, we have a painterly mix and lots of visual excitement.

steal this

These classic pieces get the seal of approval for both generations—and they can both enjoy the color jolt these bags offer with other outfits (they can't be switched here).

Dressing up (and doing it well) for certain occasions is one way of demonstrating our regard for others and for ourselves—and our daughters, of course.

Looking for Style in All the Wrong Places?

Lura picked pieces that were never meant to be on one body at one time—they have different personalities and are unflattering. The gypsy look should have never left the caravan.

"I don't feel old, nor am I treated as an old woman when I wear cool clothes."
—Lura

FOREVER COOL

As Easy as Black and White

The stylish look of these outfits owes much to their stark graphic black-and-white simplicity and clean lines. The clothing itself contributes equally to the ladies' good looks: beautiful, quality fabrics that are cut and constructed well and in a flattering style. Lura and Ann will shine at luncheons and dinners in these classic separates that are open canvases ready to be accessorized in a number of ways.

Silver Polish

Choosing silver pieces like Lura's, which has a Mexican vintage heritage, or like Ann's special silver link sixteen-inch necklace, give the women's outfits artful dimension.

steal this

Lura looks best in body-skimming (but never too loose) styles. Ann shows off her long, shapely torso in this belted safari-style jacket, which wouldn't suit Lura. The exaggerated bootleg, cuffed pant (with the necessary high-heeled sandal) that Ann can wear age- and figure-wise would not be up Lura's alley.

Patchwork Primitive
Artistic is as artistic does.

Aqua Alert
No need for a smoke signal in this outfit.

FOREVER COOL

Testing Patterns

Cynthia and daughter Malene always want to make sure they have great style to smile about. Cynthia's silk-chiffon poncho with a python pattern is in keeping with her penchant for unique clothes that don't overemphasize a generous bust line. She pairs it with easy stretch ankle-length pants that work well with a flat ballet shoe. Malene is comfortable in a sleeveless wrap top, soft cotton ombré skirt, and flat ballet shoes.

Accessory Aptitude

Glasses that read "modern" always offer 20/20 vision.

steal this

The glamorous patterns—yes! The ballet shoes . . . why not? But the rest is age appropriate on each woman.

No Flower Power
Where did this look get its roots?

Gaudy Getups
Add "ghastly" to describe the color sensibility.

FOREVER COOL

Cape Collateral

Capes serve a similar function to shawls and sweaters, providing warmth and an opportunity to layer texture and pattern. Lura's Spanish-inspired, heavily embroidered version has a vintage feel. Ann's longer cotton knit cloak has a Bedouin look. They could have worn black beneath their capes, but cream and white injects a summery, light spirit to their outfits.

Accessory Wise

Keeping the ethnic/vintage personality of the look is key. Lura's unusual handbag is loosely crocheted with a roomy black linen bag cocooned within, all suspended from a wooden anchor and handle. Both women wear vintage-inspired Mexican silver jewelry.

steal this

The ladies can trade the cape and the jewelry, and Lura could wear Ann's outfit if it was sized appropriately, but not her shoes (ouch!). Ann loves Lura's cape, bag, and shoes but would rightly pick her own age-appropriate underlayers.

167

Sugar and Spice, but Is Anything Nice?

She's nice, but her look isn't. From head to toe she needs to rethink her style ingredients.

Hazardous Hair

Those messy strands are bound to mar her vision.

Southern Exposure

The see-through gathered skirt adds pounds and pulls our gaze down to where it shouldn't be.

FOREVER COOL

Leather Luxe

Ifé's brown suede unconstructed jacket comfortably skims her frame. She achieves a sophisticated neutral palette by pairing it with a lightweight charcoal wool turtleneck and straight-leg charcoal wool slacks. Nicole is hip and sexy in her beige suede tunic dress, simply paired with a lightweight brown turtleneck and dark brown opaque tights.

Added Value

Nicole's outfit is made even more special by those gorgeous brown leather over-the-knee boots, which accentuate her long limbs. Ifé holds a roomy fabric clutch that captures our interest with an unusual puckered texture and neutral ombré coloring. Her brown suede flats, too, are perfect with her look.

steal this

Ifé's outfit is right for her age and particularly right for her figure. A woman into her fifties could wear Nicole's look, as long as she has a similar figure and great legs.

Style-Phobia Syndrome

There is nothing to fear from style but fear of style itself. Apprehension often leads to wardrobe doldrums.

FOREVER COOL

The Goods on Gray

A favorite choice for Lura and Ann, they know gray is softer than black and is a flattering neutral color that's easily worn alone or combined with other neutrals. Part of the fun of using solid neutrals is the flexibility to showcase texture. Here it's in the form of leathers and knits.

Running Wild

Ann's satchel and Lura's driving moccasins in gray python add just the spicy pattern these outfits needed.

steal this

Lura could conceivably wear Ann's outfit, in her own size. Lura's clothing is too loose and somewhat mature for Ann right now. However, if Ann or Lura is entertaining the thought of borrowing the bag or shoes, they should never wear them together in the same outfit—that would be way too much of a good thing.

Lady Who Lunches

Predictable and ubiquitous, this look (often seen in knits) ages all who subscribe to it.

Formula Dressing

Red top, black bottom. The combination started in the '80s, based on so-called "power" colors, and still maintains a stranglehold on (otherwise intelligent) ladies who lunch, politicians, TV anchors, and businesswomen.

FOREVER COOL

Modern Marvels

"Youthful," "classic," and "modern" are not empty words. Their meanings are apparent in this photograph of Portia and daughter Paige. Portia looks sleek, understated, and refined in a cashmere cardigan with fur collar over a pale gray silk T-shirt. Her classic tubular pants skim just below her waist and lightly settle on her shoe to finish the look. Paige wears an almost-black jacket and modern slim skirt in the classic knee length (less "junior" looking than a shorter version would be). Her black opaque tights do double duty, keeping her both warm and stylish.

Suitable Style

These outfits have enormous versatility, so right for many activities, from luncheons to important business functions.

steal this

The outfits are completely cross-generational. Why? These are updated and modern versions of classic jackets, sweaters, skirts, and slacks that originated in Paige's grandmother's closet; only figure and size limit borrowing potential.

Beastly Style
Faux or real, too many animal prints can make onlookers groan and growl.

Peeping Peds
Breaking with good taste by wearing dark hose with gold open-toed heels is unfortunately in keeping with the rest of her look.

FOREVER COOL

Animal Attraction

Animal prints will be with us forever, so choosing them wisely is a worthwhile investment. Here, the simple trench coat is the yin to the glamorous and exciting animal print's yang. Fabrics make a stylish difference as well: note Ellen's silky trench with a bubble-effect hem and the fun cotton velvet of Mariana's sexy skirt. Using black as an anchor color ensures that both outfits are not overdone.

steal this

"Love to!" they say, and they certainly can. The classic trench from Ellen's youth has been glamorously reinvented here as high style. With youthful appeal, it's a chic look for daughter and mom.

Judged by Her Cover

If she were a book she might never get read. Too bad the world *does* draw snap conclusions.

Color Incorrect

Yipes! Burgundy, black, and gray . . . Hasn't she read *Forever Cool?*

"I'm fifty-nine, but I feel like I'm twenty, so I have to be careful not to dress like I'm twenty!"
—Judy

FOREVER COOL

Sixties Sequel

Let's see . . . there's Jackie and Audrey, and now there's Judy and Carolyn! The next best thing to being a style icon is following in their stylish footsteps. Both coats are inspired by the chic '60s look and translated into colorful and contemporary wool models.

Booted In

Knee-high leather boots give these retro looks a modern spin and keep their legs cozy.

steal this

If your basic look is youthfully slim like Judy's, go for either of these outfits. Carolyn, because of her age, can obviously enjoy Mom's coat in her own size. The turtlenecks, boots, and gloves can be shared and mixed with lots of other separates.

chapter five
night magic

There are times in life when you really do want to make an impression or celebrate in high style—so why not go for it? It's about time we started to really enjoy life's pleasures and take the opportunities to dress to the nines for those special evening events. The problem: when the opportunity to dress up arises, we are tempted to overdo it. The trick is in learning to refrain from going over the top with what I call "goobla-glop" (too much stuff and bling), which is so prevalent in evening style. It takes an educated eye to know when bling is well done and when it's not. Another potential pitfall is conforming to the image of the "mature" woman, whose outfit says it all. Enjoy your red carpet moment by learning how to blend restraint with allure for a truly tasteful and modern style. Of course you *can* have your cake and eat it comfortably, and appropriately, too. Your daughter might happily rock in four-inch stilettos, but you may prefer to dance the night away in a lower, but just as sexy, kitten heel. She can afford a bit of décolleté, while you might want something that offers more understated, but still sensuous, coverage. Getting dressed for a big night out might be the perfect time to share in those special accessories—a jeweled purse, silky heels, or elegant drop earrings. There are many exquisite and memorable options to choose (and others to reject), as the following pictures demonstrate.

Faded Glory

Reaching a certain age doesn't mean she needs to look muted and matronly.

"For years my daughter let me pick out her clothes; now I'm letting her pick out mine."
—Susan

FOREVER COOL

Toast of the Town

Susan exhibits her full potential by wearing a feminine brown silk taffeta blouse whose empire style elongates her already tall figure. She pairs it with a multilayered skirt in a delicate and exquisite chiffon botanical print. Alexis's similarly cut dress is multilayered taupe chiffon.

Golden Opportunity

Susan's hair color and the warm yellow band at her skirt's hemline suggest gold accessories. Using this bright metallic sparingly (only in her purse) and coupling it with a burnished gold evening sandal maintains her look of refinement. Alexis's gold sandals and cascading gold earrings have an ancient Grecian effect and beautifully accompany the style of her sensuous dress.

steal this

The empire style is cross-generational, but these outfits are age appropriate for each woman. The earrings and bag will find their way to enhancing both Susan's and Alexis's wardrobes, but the four-inch height of Alexis's sandals may be an issue for Susan.

I Can and Therefore I Do

Having a good figure is a liability if
bad judgment accompanies it.

"Once I told Michelle
that she has twice the
freedom to wear what
she wants than I did at
her age in Japan. Her
reply is that she has
two hundred percent
less freedom than
her friends. I guess
that's the difference
between our two cul-
tures and generations."
—Yasue

FOREVER COOL

A Classic Spin

These two dresses are kissing cousins of the little black dress concept due to their versatility and simplicity in color and cut.

As Easy as Black and White

Yes, black accessories are the chic and modern way to go. On another day, daughter Michelle may consider a tomato-red bag for an unexpected twist to her purist black-and-white look.

steal this

Mom is still young and fit enough to wear Michelle's youthful dress. Michelle will look sophisticated and perhaps just a few years older in Yasue's outfit, but at her age, hey, who cares?

Sheer Madness . . . and Then Some!

We don't need glasses to see what we shouldn't—or to feel too dizzied by all she wears.

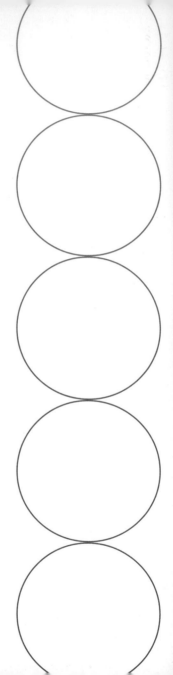

184

FOREVER COOL

Evening Stars

Ifé's full figure looks best in the unbroken line an all-black jacket and pant creates. The sequined notched collar draws our attention to her lovely face. Statuesque Nicole puts emphasis on her long, shapely legs by wearing a short 1930s-inspired layered chiffon chemise with an overall pattern of tiny velvet bows.

Silver Smarts

Nicole's accessories are the height of chic, a combo of retro style, modern simplicity, and engaging, shimmery sequined texture.

steal this

Physically different and chronologically distant, Ifé and Nicole both shine in their own way. Nicole draws on vintage style that is the stuff of some wonderful old family photos. Ifé needs modern simplicity to attain her lovely look. Both ladies are hip to this sparkling bag's wow factor.

Getting dressed for a big night out might be the perfect time to share in those special accessories.

Missing the "Miss"?

They're being polite when they say "Excuse me, ma'am," but understand some matronly looks deserve it.

Counterfeit Color

Did Judy's legs go on a sunny vacation on their own?

"Sometimes it takes feeling great in clothes to make me comfortable in my own skin. Thank God for fashion . . . it's always changing and there's something that always makes me say, 'Well, this doesn't work . . . but *this* is perfect!'"
—Judy's daughter

FOREVER COOL

Highlights and Lowlights

Judy and daughter Carolyn are both definitely camera ready with a clean evening look that creates visual excitement within a limited neutral palette via reflective fabrics, graphic metallic appliqué, and gems.

Here's Looking at You!

Note that nothing these women wear overtakes them. No bling overdose here! Like great ensemble players the chandelier earrings that decorate Judy's long neck; the short, faux diamond pair on Carolyn; her sparkling smoky gem cuff and vintage-inspired gray wool purse with incredible floral stonework; and Judy's modernist pale silver clutch all support the stylish theme.

steal this

The styles and accessories are appropriate for both age groups. But consider the demands of white slim-legged pants, as opposed to fluid wide-leg palazzos, and the age-appropriate coverage of Judy's tunic as compared with Carolyn's sleeveless version.

So Loud She Can't Hear What People Are Saying

The lurid wannabe-ethnic-print top paired with ultra-biker-chick black leather slacks shouts "tough cookie," not "Yes, I'd love a canapé!"

All That Glitters Is Not Gold

Just in case the outfit didn't speak to you, the brassy bag has the last unfortunate word.

FOREVER COOL

Golden State

Malene and Cynthia hail a taxi, but their gorgeous outfits may stop all traffic. The truly artsy vintage-look dress-and-coat outfits show how an unusual medley of vibrant color (ocher, sunflower gold, gray, brown, khaki, silver, and black), multitextured fabric, and a sophisticated print *can* be successfully and harmoniously mixed.

Time and Again

Cynthia's evening purse and black evening heels with gold chain, and Malene's ultrayellow gold heels, all hark to the '30s and contribute to the very special vintage feel.

steal this

These outfits were designed to be mixed; a sophisticated designer's eye ensured the success of this mix of patterns. Somewhat bohemian, this look is right for aspirant fashionistas of all generations. But acquiring the skill needed to assemble it well on one's own takes practice.

chapter six
speaking accessories

The accessory drawer is a happy place where mother and daughter can do the most swapping and experimenting. Accessories are fun, as they should be, and oh-so-critical to your overall look. Chosen with care, glasses, watches, shoes, bags, jewelry, headbands, belts, shawls, and scarves can pull an outfit together and bring a youthful, up-to-date feeling to the simplest attire. They can also transform one basic outfit into many looks; the result is the illusion of a larger and more diverse wardrobe.

Accessorizing well is an artful and unique visual language. Jewelry, shoes, scarves, and bags can speak quietly (diamond or pearl studs; simple black patent clutch; and heels) or boldly (oversize tortoiseshell links; large men's stainless steel watch; large red calfskin tote), depending on the message you want to send. Accessories also talk by omission: when you take the minimalist or "less is more" approach, you are making a statement, just as you are when you stack your arm high with colorful African bracelets.

Quality of workmanship, material, and design should serve as your guide in accessory decision making. These are the determining factors in why you would choose one pair of shoes or necklace or bag over another. Buy the best-quality accessories you can afford. At times you are better off spending more on accessories than on yet another outfit, especially on items you use every day, like a great pair of glasses, a special designer bag, or a beautiful watch. These pieces maintain integrity and style for years.

So what item says the most about you? Your watch—it speaks volumes about your personality and your style, basically summarizing it. For instance, a bold, masculine watch says "confident and sporty"; a dainty gold bracelet style indicates your traditional and possibly conservative outlook; a plastic Mickey Mouse watch *screams* you need a wardrobe overhaul!

Eyeglasses, too, are important and very noticeable accessories, and the face is our first focus. They tell the world how you think of yourself, so it follows that youthful and modern choices are in your best interest. Simple plastic black or tortoiseshell frames are "today"—even colors like oranges and greens can be captivating (just no silly patterns, please), as long as they flatter your coloring and facial structure. Wire and totally frameless glasses are dated on women and too aging. There's a reason why they're called "granny glasses." You rarely see a stylish younger woman wearing them. Why? When we wear frameless or wire specs, we often think they're less noticeable. A young woman sees no problem in needing glasses to read or for any other purpose, and in fact considers the plethora of gorgeous frames available today a fun, stylish accessory to be noticed by others—and so should you!

What is presented here is a very small sampling of special and everyday accessories I consider to be terrific options for mothers (your daughter will covet them—if you're feeling generous you can let her borrow these goodies) in all the various styles of dressing, from classic to ethnic. Look carefully at these items (some are featured on our models) so that when you are searching on your own, you can identify those accessories that you will love and that will work as well within each category of clothing you already own (sport, casual, dressy, etc.) as they will with the clothing you plan to buy.

Remember: accessories can make—or break—your outfit!

Buy the best-quality accessories that you can afford.

Quality of workmanship, material, and design should serve as your guide in accessory decision making.

handbags

1 Every woman needs *at least* one everyday black bag. This medium-size, roomy, and modern nylon (so lightweight) and leather example is practical and durable, modern and classic. In other words, quality construction and great style equals years of service. Long enough double handles afford over-the-shoulder ease; the bag also cinches shut for security.

2 Your *other* everyday bag should be in the brown family. This pebbled leather version won't scratch or soil easily and is supple yet rugged. It's medium size (a good proportion even for petite women), and numerous compartments make it easy to keep organized.

3 This African-inspired designer bag is a unique collector's item—perfect to add or enhance an ethnic touch in a particular outfit. Note that there are many authentic African bags to be had that are low in price and high in design value (and your purchase may lend support to talented people in an impoverished country).

4 As an alternative to your day-to-day black bag (or even to be used every day), patent is perfection: it's lightweight, continues to look new for many years, and offers a practical solution for inclement weather. For those who love zippers and multiple pockets for design interest and usefulness, this model hits nirvana. (page 133)

This small leather bag (just four by five inches) is ready for its close-up. Sleek and sturdy in shiny, tomato-red leather, it holds essentials while dressing up a jean outfit or suit. Here is your opportunity for creative color play (e.g., pair this with bright orange to achieve a wow effect).

A collector's dream find, this part-vintage (the carved ivory top) small pouch purse has a one-of-a-kind look. Needless to say, it is a conversation piece in the best sense of the term: it will break the ice at any party and is the piece that can make an outfit.

A straw bag is an accessory must-have for summer. Whether you prefer more neutral beige and rustic French market totes (named after its function for shoppers in French open-air markets and stalls) or this more styled tote version (sixteen by twelve inches), any bag of this type is a summer classic and wardrobe staple. (page 45)

Incredibly beautiful and intricate beadwork, in a nod to the craftsmanship of eastern India, makes this clutch a highlight of any dressy outfit. (page 155)

A bag with personality and humor (without ever being silly!) is worth the purchase. This gem (the size of a very small flowerpot) will make your little black dress or possibly a cream linen outfit even more special.

A plain black satin evening bag will do—but why not go the extra mile with great style? This clutch is beautifully embroidered with jet-black beads that glisten under the stars. (page 163)

jewelry

The central pendant, secured by an unexpected, modern band of coiled ribbon strands, is a lovely example of eastern Indian design using characteristic gems and colors, with details often fashioned of twenty-two-karat gold.

Multiple strands of grass-green jade are twisted into a thick strand of a necklace that would grace a simple sweater with a jewel neckline (plain and round) or an open-necked blouse in high style. All eyes will also be drawn to the hand adorned by this stunning peridot and white gold ring.

This Native American multi-strand coral and silver necklace will make its important presence known at the collar of any outfit. This piece is by a modern artist, but its basic beadwork is the stuff of generations before and is usually found in the form of longer strands. The necklaces are bought both for their value as collectibles as well as their intrinsic beauty.

African beaded necklaces (like the aforementioned bags) are rich in beauty and don't require deep pockets to purchase. Think of these on a plain white cotton tee paired with all-white jeans. A huge aesthetic bang for your buck!

More is more . . . when you stack a slew of these gorgeous, inexpensive African bracelets up one arm. Go ahead! Stacking shows these beauties off to their best advantage.

1

2

3

4

1 This playful, long plastic chain necklace would add fresh, youthful spirit to any look. It exemplifies the graphic power and simplicity of the loop. Likewise, those graphic painted enamel bangles (preferably stacked for visual impact) would add tons of colorful pizzazz.

2 Apple green and citrus orange: two colors that are as undoubtedly cheery as they are modern. Here the palette is shown off on two handsome leather and silver cuffs. (page 137)

3 These lightweight Bakelite bangles (circa 1930s) would add color and unique charm, when stacked on one arm, to a casual or dressier outfit. (page 45)

4 Silver cuffs, like these two three-inch examples, are all you need to make a silver statement. Wearing just one important piece such as this, and no other jewelry (or perhaps wearing it only with small diamond studs), will maintain a minimalist vibe.

This silver design—a twist on the classic sixteen-inch chain—falls just below your neck and would grace an open-collared blouse or shirt, or a jewel-necked sweater. It would also dress up a T-shirt, adding instant style magic. (page 163)

Here is a gorgeous example of a vintage Mexican bracelet. It is comparatively affordable, very lightweight, and a great way to add ethnic silver sparkle that would imbue an outfit with artistic personality. (page 163)

This vintage Mexican necklace can be that one important piece on your outfit or can be paired with a cuff. Ethnic pieces are perfect worn alone or in quantity, as opposed to bling elements—think Frida Kahlo, who kept it artfully authentic, and without the flash.
(page 163)

A beautiful alternative to classic pearls, this antique glass sixteen-inch necklace's transparency gives it unique and interesting dimension, making it an especially captivating adornment.

A fob chain looks classic. Here, it is interpreted in a modern way—this sixteen-inch silver necklace can surely be your everyday piece. There's little it wouldn't look right with.

Lucky enough to find this charming bracelet? Perhaps on a trip out west, as its chain is chock-full of silver Western-themed charms, from a Native American chief's bonnet to a wagon wheel. Though they can be noisy, pieces like this are classic no matter what the theme or decibel level!

A large (yes, man-size) silver watch can be your stylish and very utilitarian everyday watch no matter how petite you or your wrist may be. It says "strong and vital" in a youthful way (pass on a watch with added bling embellishment; it sends the opposite message).

Rugged, sporty watches, which can keep you carefree and well equipped from the gym to flying the skies or exploring the deep sea, are also a great stylish look. Think of them for all your sporty outfits. (pages 19 and 27)

shoes

Wellington-type rubber rain boots (named after the first duke of Wellington) are often affectionately called "wellies" and certainly qualify as classics. Green has been most popular through the years (it has become a basic, like black), but wellies now come in a rainbow of fashion colors (avoid overly cutesy prints, however).

When you can combine utility, comfort, and classicism with modern style, you go, girl! These low riding-style shiny black leather boots (a look that is akin to patent) are also endowed with comfortable, thick rubber soles. They're so good for brisk walking on city pavements that you may never go back to thin leather soles.

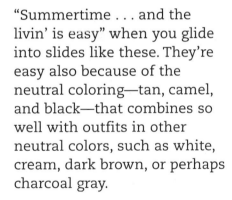

"Summertime . . . and the livin' is easy" when you glide into slides like these. They're easy also because of the neutral coloring—tan, camel, and black—that combines so well with outfits in other neutral colors, such as white, cream, dark brown, or perhaps charcoal gray.

Classic loafers in rubber-soled brown suede (or leather), as shown, and in basic black are de rigueur for everyday classic style and premium comfort. They can be multiseasonal (yes, even suede for summer, and brown and black worn with white). Loafers come in a multitude of styles, and also as moccasins (meaning they have no visible sole). Once you own some basics, treat yourself to more pairs in colors like tan, bright orange, yellow, and olive green.

So feminine and comfortable... these shimmery slides have a vintage look but are thoroughly modern. (page 167)

the total package

Stunning in her classic simplicity, the ageless beauty knows the key to lasting loveliness: playing stylish, youthful clothes against a clean, minimally made-up face and healthy, free-flowing hair. She recognizes that the innocence of a natural, uncalculated look is so charming and disarming—and provides balance to a carefully considered outfit, perhaps especially one that's high fashion.

The origins of this effortless look are in part European; Mediterranean women in particular seem to know that clean skin with just a touch of lip color and longish, tousled hair that you can easily run your fingers through is sexy and sensuous at every age. Europeans are not as quick to "go under the knife" either, instead tending to their skin with loving, but noninvasive, care. Yet there's also an all-American tradition of keeping hair simple and the face minimally made up (think Grace Kelly in anything; a young Ali MacGraw in *Love Story* and *The Getaway*; or Lena Horne at every age and stage of her life). Study any Ralph Lauren ad to see what I mean, and while you're at it, check out his wife, Ricki, whose look so exemplifies his ethic (and mine!). Ralph Lauren is a master at interpreting the slightly untamed, but always thoroughbred, fresh-faced look.

Happily, many women in this country—your daughters, perhaps—have enthusiastically rediscovered and embraced this style, and with good reason: it's easy and beautiful. Chloë Sevigny, Halle Berry, Jennifer Connelly, Penélope Cruz, and Kate Winslet are youthful big-screen examples of fashionable women who have chosen to keep their skin and hair looking natural, with occasional evening drama on their lips or eyes. Meredith Vieira, Joan Baez, Martha Stewart, Lauren Hutton, Jamie Lee Curtis, and Ann Curry are boomer (and older) women who "keep it real" to flattering and youthful effect. Let's take a cue from these women, and our real-life daughters—at least the ones who have been listening to Mother (Mother Nature, that is).

Best Face Forward

Isn't it both liberating and reassuring to understand that a bare face enhanced with just a hint of cosmetic assistance is fresh and youthful? The best way to achieve this natural look starts with ample (daytime, if possible) light and a good makeup mirror, necessities for women both young and older. They tell you the truth like a trusted confidant. A mirror with five-X (or higher) magnification is best for seeing all flaws and features clearly. Magnification allows for more meticulous application of makeup—and keeps you from overdoing it—as well as precise brow shaping and plucking that errant hair.

Should you choose to use foundation, select a

luminescent, sheer liquid that reflects light, deflecting flaws while allowing your own skin to shine through, freckles and all. Or consider forgoing the base in favor of moisturizer and a tawny-colored blush or bronzer judiciously applied to cheeks, temples, and tip of the nose to add a look of sun-kissed health and vitality so emblematic of youthful energy.

Go back a bit; remember when colorful eye shadow, frosted lipstick, and fake eyelashes were de rigueur for evenings out? Well . . . times have changed, *at least for us*. Women in their twenties and thirties can play more with theatrical night-time makeup if they want. It's not an issue if heavy makeup makes them look a bit older than they are. But that's not true for us as we age. The minimal and more natural approach described above is appropriate for evening as well as day-time. It is not mandatory to wear more makeup at night. If you want to indulge in some drama for special events, accentuate lips or eyes but don't play up both. It's about balance. Think *either* red lipstick *or* a smoky eye!

Everyday enhancing of your eyes is as important as pampering your skin—after all, eyes are meant to be expressive. Neutral eye shadows in beige, taupe, and gray flatter most eye colors (the exception to the neutral palette being a beautiful, subtle lilac shadow with green eyes). A couple of passes over your lashes with sable brown or black mascara and your eyes are done.

Lipstick or gloss two shades deeper than your own lip color is a becoming finale. Caution: you may not necessarily be so pretty in pink, contrary to a plethora of advice claiming that this highly specific color is the savior of all women of a certain age. No matter how old you are, an outright pink should relate to something that you are wearing (a pink jacket, perhaps?), and that holds for other distinct colors as well. A tawny lipstick tone is the most universal shade, a good neutral for the modern woman of any age. Couple that purchase with a good lip liner pencil that will either match your chosen lipstick or be lighter than it (darker lip liner is so yesterday, even for your daughter). Apply your liner first, following your lip's contours, to prevent your lipstick from bleeding. Last, remember not to immediately eat up your lipstick by pressing your lips inward (we do it without thinking!); use tissue to blot instead.

A tawny lipstick tone is the most universal shade,
a good neutral for the modern woman of any age.

Good lipstick can be found in every price range, from drugstore brands to high-end department store lines. This means you can afford to experiment until you find the right neutral tone for your coloring. Note that names can be deceiving: "Very Berry" has as much chance of being brownish as it does reddish. "Caramel" might be coral, or it could be beige. When shopping, focus on the sample swatches and ignore their seductive monikers.

Speaking of lovely mouths, can your teeth be whiter and straighter? Nothing is more of a deal maker than a bright, clean smile. Years of coffee, tea, and red wine drinking can leave stubborn stains on your not-so-pearly whites. There's good news in the form of over-the-counter and high-tech professional whitening products and processes widely available at every price point. Straightening and veneer procedures have become less invasive in recent years as well. Consider tooth enhancement as part of your new wardrobe, and you'll have plenty to grin about!

A Finished Touch

It's been said that God is in the details. Your nails, as much as anything, reveal your attitude and personal style. Clean and natural is the modern message. Short, slightly rounded buffed nails, with cuticles pushed back, form the perfect base for a clear coat of a pale beige polish. Beware the "French manicure" advertised at ubiquitous corner nail salons. They are so rarely done correctly they may be best avoided altogether, as are absurdly long nails, extensions, gimmicky designs, and colors that clash with your outfit. Hands themselves should be protected just like the skin on your face—with daily applications of moisturizer and sunscreen. Remember, as you

> **Nothing is more of a deal maker than a bright, clean smile.**

> **Remember as you age, your hands can tell your story. . . .**

age, your hands can tell your story. . . . Are you still that very active woman who projects unhampered chic?

The Mane Line

A fresh face cries out for healthy, shiny hair in a modern and sensuous style I call "studied messiness"—effortless and unself-conscious. Actresses such as Uma Thurman, Rita Wilson, Charlotte Rampling, and Jacqueline Bisset are good examples (within their respective generations) of the look. Witness the adorable models in the pages of the J.Crew catalog, and you'll see Gen Y examples that may immediately win you over. There's no need for extreme hair or overuse of product to look amazing.

Today there are many practical (and pretty) items that help keep hair looking young. Accoutrements like leather or faux-tortoise hair bands keep longish hair feminine and casually understated; covered bands are must-haves for classic ponytails, great for on-the-go daytime style. Invisible hairpins hold chignons or gentle upsweeps in place, which are so lovely and easy for evening. None of these styles requires weekly pilgrimages

> **Tousled hair that you can easily run your fingers through is sensuous and sexy at any age.**

to the "beauty parlor" to get "done." But, hey, a visit to the salon for regular maintenance, of course, should be an enjoyable and relaxing ritual.

If you are lucky enough to have a healthy head full of spun silver or white, embrace it! A well-cared-for mane of shimmery gray is show-stoppingly modern and luxe. But not all gray is the same; it can be aging. For those who want to cover salt and pepper, or ramp up existing color, consider a tone with layers of differentiated color. Single-process color doesn't achieve subtle variations. Look at a child's untouched tresses: they have many shades and tones, including low- and highlights. A talented and experienced pro (find a good one!) can help you achieve the authentic shading you need: brown hair can range from oak to walnut; blond hair may be an array of golden hues from pale yellow to strawberry or caramel; redheads might have honey strands mixed in with a head full of mahogany.

Ultimately, modern and radiant beauty for baby boomers (and their daughters) is about taking care of what you've got and treating it like the precious commodity it is. It's beauty from the inside out, if you will. You can face the world head-on, and even turn approving heads in the process, if you keep it simple and natural, eat your vegetables (wink, wink), drink lots of water, and get your exercise. So there: all things *your* mother told you, and advice you might extol to your daughter—or is your daughter now advising you? With good reason—it works!

A fresh face cries out for healthy, shiny hair in a modern and sensuous style I call "studied messiness"—effortless and unself-conscious.

Ultimately, modern and radiant beauty for baby boomers (and their daughters) is about taking care of what you've got and treating it like the precious commodity it is.

observing style in motion: sources of inspiration

Your daughters—and the younger generations in general—are increasingly influenced by popular culture. Today's style is so informed by what's going on in "the street" and on movies and television. As simple as it sounds, having a genuine interest in the world and staying curious reward the constant observer with valuable aesthetic stimulation and better visual values. It's fun and important for you to keep in step. Consciously evaluate what is good and bad on both young and older women (it's all out there)—including those on the silver and flat screens.

In time, you will become more skilled at discerning fleeting trends from lasting style ideas, beautifully made clothing and mediocre copies, striking silhouettes and unflattering cuts. What made you turn around quickly and stare at that woman who just passed you?

And then there's the option of sitting at home or in a theater watching a movie. Movies offer a particularly helpful universe of historical and current style information and are one of my favorite sources of inspiration and ideas—I recommend them for the sheer power of their visual information and aesthetic education. Here's a gathering of some that will help train your eye and stimulate your thinking. All this can be part of an engaging

> ## What made you turn around quickly and stare at that woman who just passed you?

discussion between you and your daughter ("Wow, wasn't that an incredible dress Gwyneth wore?").

Movie watching is not so much about drawing literal inspiration as observing how style expresses personality. Style is an element of cinema that costume designers work very hard at in partnership with directors. When I was a costume designer I strived to strengthen each character's defining traits and attitudes through their dress so that audiences would know more about them even if they said little or nothing. That dedication and care on the part of professional costume artists is why films are such rich wells of information. A film like *Something's Gotta Give* shows two generations of women (mother and daughter), played by Diane Keaton and Amanda Peet, beautifully dressed in modern yet classic style—you can tell a lot about them simply by looking at their clothes: they are well educated and share common traditional values but aren't afraid to be independent. All that just from looking at their outfits!

Many films intentionally use fashion as part of their narrative and even give it center stage in the role of a character. For example, *Clueless* celebrates fashion experimentation and youthful exuber-

Movie watching is not so much about drawing literal inspiration as observing how style expresses personality.

Ralph Lauren made iconic actors and actresses guideposts for his classic signature style.

ance. Clothes are very much part of how we are perceived and judged by the world, and no film makes that point clearer. Another example is the genius work of director Christopher Guest along with his designer Durinda Wood; they are masters at lampooning women who forgo contemporary, refined style in favor of silliness, hypersexuality, or DIY craft-store looks. The costumes created for *A Mighty Wind, For Your Consideration,* and *Best in Show,* perfectly capture the woman of a certain age indulging in either a dowdy or absurd cacophony of colors, prints, and general no-nos.

Cinema classics (*Two for the Road* comes to mind) and the stylish stars of the past have long inspired both Hollywood actors and New York fashion designers. Fred and Ginger, and Lombard and Gable, still have an impact on runway and red carpet looks for men and women. One only has to think of George Clooney and Gwen Stefani gliding past the paparazzi at an awards show to understand where their latest looks originally came from. Ralph Lauren made iconic actors and actresses guideposts for his classic signature style. Master designer Ralph Lauren's great influ-

ences must include people like Cary Grant, Gary Cooper, Marlene Dietrich, Audrey Hepburn, and the work of Hollywood photographer Slim Aarons, who captured the privileged at play better than anyone of the era.

Then there are period costume dramas that wash over us with stunning wardrobes—with these films we can be inspired by color and texture and, if we are able, undertake the difficult task of translating what we see into our everyday wardrobe. *Memoirs of a Geisha, Marie Antoinette,* and the HBO drama *John Adams* are just a few amazing examples of skilled costume designers at work. The fabrics, colors, lines, and embellishments are thrilling to study, and these features are the reason historical dramas are able to transport us, briefly, to another place and time. After the lights go up, consider how to carry on those aesthetic inspirations in a modern way.

At seven, Daisy Mae is getting older, but she feels more like a puppy and is still eager to brush up on some new fashion tricks. Besides, everyone knows that seven is the new six! Let's loosen those old style chains while engaging the younger generations . . . and have the best style years (and "treats") of our lives.

Magazine Stand

Many fashion and lifestyle magazines exemplify modern, classic, yet hip style in dress and decor (so related!). These publications hold themselves to such a high standard that looking at them is educational and stimulating, even if you cannot afford the clothing, accessories, and furnishings shown in their pages. If you are able to identify the latest colors, textures, and trends that are right for you, you can approximate or capture the refinement and modernity when choosing your own (more affordable) selections. Why not open their pages?

Allure

Reliable, realistic, and modern advice about hair, makeup, and fashion trends.

Elle

Young but sophisticated, with a plethora of adventurous, trendsetting ideas.

Harper's Bazaar

This fashion standard shows all the latest styles but also interprets them for specific age groups.

Martha Stewart Living

Not a fashion magazine of course, but still a great resource for inspiration and ideas, color combinations, and good taste—all presented through the lens of the best photographers and the eyes of the most highly trained stylists. The level of visuals in the magazine is worth the cover price alone.

More

This magazine, specifically for women forty and over, provides encouraging news stories and lifestyle and health information.

O, the Oprah Magazine

Realistic, modern style and fashion advice for today's woman of any age, and so much more.

Real Simple

Often includes fashion features that are contemporary but not too fashion forward—plus sound style advice for both home and closet.

Self

Great information about modern sport style—as well as reliable health, dietary, and fitness information.

Town and Country

Offers an in-depth peek into the world of the very wealthy. Upscale fashion, travel, and interior design. Inspiring, to say the least!

Travel and Leisure

Beautiful photographs of travel destinations and accommodations as well as up-to-date information about stylish travel clothing, luggage, and accessories.

Vogue

The authority on fashion trends—while most of what is shown may not be right for you as is, you can glean color, palette, cut, and fit trends that you will be able to translate to your own closet.

W

You'll be clued in to what is hip and happening on the runways, but not necessarily what should be hanging in your closet. Useful for inspiration and fun fodder for cocktail party chatter.

A genuine interest in the world and staying curious rewards the constant observer.

shopping around

The clothing world is at your fingertips—you no longer have to be short-changed by your local lack of mercantile choices. You can seek out and purchase a wide range of options thanks to the Internet and mail-order catalogs. Excursions to retail hotbeds like New York City, Los Angeles, Paris, London, and Milan are also exciting and very immediate ways to absorb firsthand inspiration on the street, in museums, and at cutting-edge boutiques and long-standing stylish retailers.

An educated eye should be able to assess what will stand the test of time and what won't—that's where shopping becomes a little bit of a challenge. Yet the more critically you look at how a thing is designed and constructed, the more you learn. The woman who confines herself to only low-priced stores is the woman who will never learn about workmanship, who will miss the benefit of being exposed to original design, and who may miss out on that special item she may covet.

Your purchasing power needn't make high-end stores off-limits. Consider sales for that extraordinary piece of clothing or accessory that you think is beyond your budget. Shop smart. Develop a relationship with salespeople and tell them when you are interested in something that is beyond your means at full price. She or he will call you if it goes on sale—that's what is called intelligent customer service.

Here is a carefully edited list of retailers, catalogs, designers, and online purveyors whose looks and principles offer great examples of what's shown in this book. Their items have earned my respect and admiration. None are "specialty" stores in the sense of catering to middle-aged women. If not in their stores, some retailers offer larger, petite, or other special sizes online. So mothers and daughters, let's partake in a time-honored tradition that can even bring us closer together—let's go shopping!

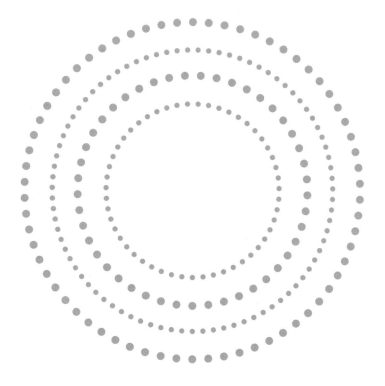

Adidas

www.shopadidas.com
Sportswear available at free-standing stores and sporting good retailers throughout the U.S.

Agnès B.

www.agnesb.com/us
Ultrasimple, casual women and men's clothing in free-standing stores located in major cities across the U.S. and internationally.

Ann Taylor

www.anntaylor.com
Casual, professional, and dressy clothing, accessories, and shoes in freestanding stores located throughout the U.S.

Armani Collezioni

www.armanicollezioni.com
Professional and dressy clothes in freestanding stores and fine department stores located throughout the U.S.

Banana Republic

www.bananarepublic.com
Sporty, casual, professional, and dressy clothes, accessories, and shoes in freestanding stores located throughout the U.S.

Bare Necessities

www.barenecessities.com
Online source for fine lingerie and bras.

Barneys New York

www.barneys.com
Fashion-forward clothing, accessories, and shoes. Free-standing stores in major cities across the U.S.

BCBG MAX AZRIA

www.bcbg.com
Trendy, casual to dressy clothing, accessories, and shoes in freestanding stores nationwide, and at Saks Fifth Avenue and Bloomingdale's.

Bergdorf Goodman

www.bergdorfgoodman.com
New York's finest department store, offering a wide range of modern, trendy, and classic clothing, accessories, and shoes.

Bliss

www.blissworld.com
Catalog and freestanding stores for cosmetics and hair care products, plus spa products and some casual, body-conscious clothing.

Bluefly

www.bluefly.com
Online resource for designer clothing, accessories, and shoes at discount prices.

Bra Smyth

www.brasmyth.com
Complete collection of bras and some swimwear, including hard-to-find styles and sizes, in their catalog, online, and in freestanding stores.

Brooks Brothers

www.brooksbrothers.com
A variety of casual to dressy classic clothing in freestanding stores located throughout the U.S.

Burberry

www.burberry.com
High-fashion, casual to dressy clothing, accessories, and shoes, located in freestanding stores and fine department stores throughout the U.S. and internationally.

Calvin Klein

www.calvinklein.com
Modern, luxe clothes, from casual and professional to dressy, in freestanding stores and in fine department stores nationwide and internationally.

Cartier

www.cartier.com
Fine watches and jewelry in freestanding stores and department stores across the U.S.

Coach

www.coach.com
Shoes and accessories, and some clothes, available in freestanding stores and fine department stores throughout the U.S.

Cole Haan

www.colehaan.com
Accessories and shoes available at freestanding stores and fine department stores across the U.S.

eBay to

www.ebay.com
Online auction source for an unpredictable assortment of new overstock items, recent but gently used clothing, accessories, and vintage designer duds, often at greatly reduced prices.

Eileen Fisher

www.eileenfisher.com
Unconstructed, casual clothing, accessories, and shoes at freestanding stores and fine department stores nationwide.

Emilio Pucci 🪝🪝🪝🪝

www.emiliopucci.com
High-fashion clothing, shoes, and accessories known for their distinct and colorful prints in freestanding stores and fine department stores nationwide and internationally.

Etro 🪝🪝🪝🪝

High-fashion clothing, accessories, and shoes known for their distinct and colorful prints, in freestanding stores and department stores nationwide.

Footsmart 🪝

www.footsmart.com
Catalog of shoe comfort products, such as heel protectors and sole pads.

Fred Segal

www.fredsegal.com
Trendy casual to dressy clothing, accessories, and shoes in freestanding California stores.

Gap

www.gap.com
Casual clothing, accessories, and shoes at freestanding stores across the U.S. and internationally.

Giorgio Armani
🪝🪝🪝🪝

www.armani.com
Dressy clothing, accessories, and shoes in freestanding stores and fine department stores throughout the U.S.

Gorsuch 🪝🪝🪝

www.gorsuchltd.com
Catalog and freestanding Colorado stores for fine ski and après-ski wear, and casual and dressy clothing appropriate for ski country.

Gucci 🪝🪝🪝🪝

www.gucci.com
High-end accessories, shoes, and high-style clothing in freestanding stores and fine department stores located throughout the U.S. and internationally.

Henry Lehr

(212) 274-9921
Known for jeans, but also offers a range of casual clothing and accessories in freestanding stores in New York and Connecticut.

Hermès

www.hermes.com
Ultra-high-end leather handbags and accessories, and
stylish clothing (often with an
equestrian and classic core), at
freestanding stores located
throughout the U.S.; select
items available at fine department stores.

InStyle.com
 to

shopping.instyle.com
InStyle magazine offers a com-
prehensive one-stop online
store that aggregates casual,
professional, and dressy clothing and accessories from a
variety of designers, retailers,
and online catalogs.

James Perse ⌂ ⌂

www.jamesperse.com
Casual clothes in upscale
department stores across the
country and internationally.

JC Penney ⌂

www.jcpenney.com
National department store
with some lower-priced interpretations of designer clothing, shoes, and accessories,
most notably from Ralph Lauren, designing under a brand
called American Living.

J.Crew ⌂ **to** ⌂ ⌂

www.jcrew.com
Classic-with-a-twist casual,
professional, and dressy
clothes, accessories, and shoes
available at freestanding
stores throughout the U.S.

Jil Sander ⌂ ⌂ ⌂ ⌂

www.jilsander.com
High-fashion clothing, accessories, and shoes available at
freestanding stores and fine
department stores.

Jimmy Choo ⌂ ⌂ ⌂ ⌂

www.jimmychoo.com
High-fashion shoes and bags
at freestanding stores and in
fine department stores in the
U.S. and internationally.

Kate Spade
⌂ ⌂ **to** ⌂ ⌂ ⌂

www.katespade.com
Fun, whimsical handbags,
shoes, accessories and clothing available at freestanding
stores and fine department
stores nationwide.

KORS Michael Kors
⌂ ⌂ ⌂

www.michaelkors.com
Classic-with-a-twist clothing,
accessories, and shoes at freestanding stores and fine
department stores nationwide.

Lacoste ⌂ ⌂

www.lacoste.com
Sporty and casual clothes at
freestanding stores and
department stores throughout
the U.S., and internationally.

Loro Piana ⌂ ⌂ ⌂ ⌂

www.loropiana.com
Ultraluxe Italian cashmere and
other fine fabrics, mainly
casual and sport clothing,
including accessories and
shoes, in freestanding stores
and fine department stores in
the U.S. and internationally.

Lucky Brand Jeans

www.luckybrandjeans.com
Jeans and casual, funky, retro-inspired clothing in freestanding stores and department stores across the U.S.

Manolo Blahnik

www.manoloblahnik.com
Fine shoes at freestanding stores in New York, and fine department stores nationwide and internationally.

Marina Rinaldi

www.maxmarafashion.com
Casual, professional, and dressy plus sizes at freestanding stores and fine department stores throughout the U.S. and internationally.

Marni

www.marni.com
High-fashion clothing, shoes, and accessories in freestanding stores and fine department stores across the U.S. and internationally.

Max Mara

www.maxmarafashion.com
Casual, professional, and dressy clothes, shoes, and accessories at freestanding stores and fine department stores throughout the U.S. and internationally.

Mikimoto

www.mikimoto.com
Fine pearls at freestanding stores and fine department and jewelry stores throughout the U.S. and internationally.

Miu Miu

www.miumiu.com
High-fashion and trendy women's clothing, accessories, and shoes at freestanding stores and fine department stores across the U.S. and internationally.

Moschino

www.moschino.com
High-fashion Italian women's clothing at freestanding stores and fine department stores nationwide and internationally.

Neiman Marcus

www.neimanmarcus.com
Fine department store with an assortment of casual, professional, and dressy clothes, located nationwide.

Net-a-Porter
 to

www.net-a-porter.com
Internet source for designer clothing.

Nikewomen

www.nike.com/nikewomen
Sportswear and footwear online, at Nike stores, and at specialty and department stores nationwide and internationally.

Nine West Shoes

www.ninewest.com
Casual, professional, and dressy shoes and handbags at freestanding stores and department stores located throughout the U.S. and internationally.

Nordstrom

www.nordstrom.com
Department store with an assortment of casual, professional, and dressy clothes, located nationwide.

Piazza Sempione

www.piazzasempione.com
Stylish casual, professional, and dressy clothing available at fine department stores nationwide and internationally.

Prada

www.prada.com
High-fashion Italian clothing, accessories, and shoes at freestanding stores and fine department stores nationwide and internationally.

Puma

www.puma.com
Sport clothing and accessories available at freestanding, department, and specialty stores nationwide and internationally.

Ralph Lauren

www.polo.com
Casual, professional, and dressy classical style—with a twist—these clothes, accessories, and shoes are available at freestanding stores and department stores nationwide and internationally.

Lauren

to

Includes large sizes

RLX

to

The sportswear division

Rebecca Collins Jewelry

www.rebeccacollins
jewelry.com
Bold, artistic jewelry available at Neiman Marcus.

Robert Clergerie Shoes

www.robertclergerie.com
Trendy women's shoes available at freestanding stores and fine department stores nationwide and internationally.

Rolex

www.rolex.com
Fine watches available at freestanding stores and fine department and jewelry stores throughout the U.S. and internationally.

Saks Fifth Avenue

www.saksfifthavenue.com
Fine department store with an assortment of casual, professional, and dressy clothes, accessories, and shoes located nationwide.

Searle

www.searlenyc.com
High-end stylish clothing (especially outerwear), shoes, and accessories from casual to dressy at freestanding stores nationwide.

Shopbop

www.shopbop.com
Online source for a variety of designer clothing, accessories, and shoes.

Spanx ♟♟

www.spanx.com
Fine lingerie and shapewear at department and specialty stores nationwide.

Sportmax ♟♟

www.maxmarafashion.com
Casual clothes at freestanding stores and fine department stores throughout the U.S. and internationally.

Talbots ♟

www.talbots.com
Conservative casual, professional, and dressy clothing, shoes, and accessories, at freestanding stores nationwide.

Target ♟

www.target.com
National department store with some lower-priced interpretations of designer clothing, accessories, and shoes, most notably by Isaac Mizrahi.

Temple St. Clair
♟♟♟♟

www.templestclair.com
Fine gemstone and gold jewelry at Saks Fifth Avenue and fine jewelry stores nationwide.

Theory ♟♟

www.theory.com
Modern clothing, and some shoes and accessories, at freestanding stores in major U.S. cities and fine department stores in the U.S. and internationally.

Tod's ♟♟♟♟

www.tods.com
Understated yet ultrachic handbags, shoes (especially the driving moccasin), accessories, and some clothing in freestanding stores located throughout the U.S. and internationally; also available at fine department stores.

Tory Burch ♟♟♟

www.toryburch.com
Trendy, modern clothing, shoes, and accessories available at freestanding stores and fine department stores nationwide and internationally.

TSE

www.tsecashmere.com
Top-quality cashmere classics
and high-fashion clothing
available at freestanding
stores and fine department
stores in the U.S. and
internationally.

Vince

Modern casual clothes available at fine department stores
nationwide.

Wolford

www.wolford.com
Fine hosiery available at freestanding stores and fine
department stores nationwide
and internationally.

Zoran

www.saksfifthavenue.com
Modern, minimalist clothing
available at Saks Fifth Avenue.

special thanks!

To the intrepid mothers and daughters who took valuable time from work and studies, as well as traveled via trains and planes to pose and smile for me.

To Aliza Fogelson, my editor, who has seen everything my eyes would miss, and for her invaluable advice, intuitive guidance, and enthusiasm for this book. To the rest of the Clarkson Potter team for all their efforts.

To Karen Kelly for helping give form to my ideas and philosophy on the written page, and for being a wise pal while always ready to share a good laugh.

To my agent, Marcy Posner, for being my advocate.

To Nick Saraco for capturing the warm spirit of each mother-daughter duo in his "stylishly" candid photos and for putting up with the difficult schedule this project required.

To Lura and Ann, a mother and daughter whose friendship has been extraordinary and whose belief in my talent and skill bolsters me daily.

And, of course, thanks to my husband, John, for his love and support, and yes, even for serving as my only assistant on weekend days. You made this book possible.